PRAISE FOR
THE OTHER SIDE OF BEAUTY

"Leah's message and her whole ministry is, in a word: revolutionary. In an era of 'liberation' we've never had more women (or men) experience life in chains: the chains of negative self image, unhealthy comparison, hatred of their own bodies, false notions of success, or poverty of purpose. Leah is on the front line in the revolution against the emptiness of this age. Join her. Buy two of these books and give one away!"

— Chris Stefanick, founder and president of Real Life Catholic

"*The Other Side of Beauty* is a thought-provoking journey into the depths of one of our deepest desires—to behold beauty and become one with it. Through her personal experience, wisdom, and humor, Leah Darrow inspires the reader to the authentic love and beauty found in Jesus Christ. I laughed, I cried, and I thoroughly enjoyed this book!"

— Sister Miriam James Heidland, SOLT Catholic
speaker and author of *Loved As I Am*

"In *The Other Side of Beauty* Leah Darrow so clearly cuts through the lies of the culture about 'beauty,' and presents the wonderful truth of God's beauty. Leah's life experiences and her witness of hope will inspire every young woman who picks up this book to remember who they are as God's daughters and the radiant life for which they were made!"

— Jackie Francois Angel, speaker, recording artist, and author of *Forever*

"Leah Darrow uses her experience in the beauty industry to help the women of our culture see what *true* beauty looks like."

— Jennifer Fulwiler, host of *The Jennifer Fulwiler Show*
and author of *Something Other than God*

THE
OTHER
SIDE OF
BEAUTY

THE
OTHER
SIDE OF
BEAUTY

Embracing God's Vision for
Love and True Worth

LEAH DARROW

NELSON
BOOKS
An Imprint of Thomas Nelson

HarperCollins
PUBLISHERS
Since 1817

Published in Nashville, Tennessee, by Nelson Books, an imprint of Thomas Nelson. Nelson Books and Thomas Nelson are registered trademarks of HarperCollins Christian Publishing, Inc.

Published in association with the literacy agency of Wolgemuth & Associates, Inc.

The Never List™ is a trademark of Beautycounter and is used with permission.

Thomas Nelson titles may be purchased in bulk for educational, business, fund-raising, or sales promotional use. For information, please e-mail SpecialMarkets@ThomasNelson.com.

ISBN 978-0-7180-90739 (eBook)

Library of Congress Cataloging-in-Publication Data

ISBN 978-0-7180-90661
Names: Darrow, Leah, 1979- author.
Title: The other side of beauty : embracing God's vision for love and true worth / Leah Darrow.
Description: Nashville : Thomas Nelson, 2017. | Includes bibliographical references.
Identifiers: LCCN 2017021437 | ISBN 9780718090661
Subjects: LCSH: Christian women--Religious life. | Beauty, Personal--Religious aspects--Christianity.
Classification: LCC BV4527 .D355 2017 | DDC 248.8/43--dc23 LC record available at https://lccn.loc.gov/2017021437

Printed in the United States of America

17 18 19 20 21   LSC   10 9 8 7 6 5 4 3 2 1

To you, O Lord, for your mercy.

Jesus, I trust in you!

The sweetest thing in all my life has been the longing . . . to find the place where all the beauty came from.

—C. S. LEWIS,
TILL WE HAVE FACES

CONTENTS

INTRODUCTION

Pick Me! Pick Me!

REMEMBER THAT FEELING YOU GOT IN GRADE school whenever you were waiting for two captains to pick their teams for a game of kickball or some other team sport? I recall standing up against the brick school wall, anxious, praying to God that I would be picked first . . . or at least not last. Being picked meant something. It told people that you were worth something, that you were valued.

Growing up, I was one of those kids who had gotten all my height before everyone else did. I was five foot seven by the time I was twelve years old, but for reasons that escape logic, it was cool to be short in those days. I was tall and gangly and towered over my classmates, so I was left awkwardly trying to make myself shorter so I could hear the conversations between other classmates and fit in.

I wanted to belong, badly. I wanted to be chosen. I longed for a group to ask me to sit with them at lunch or to hear my name called first for a team sport—something, anything that would make me feel valued. I craved those moments of validation, and that grade-school craving never left.

Years later, though I was far past grade school, that same anxious feeling returned as I found myself standing in front of Tyra Banks, praying that she would pick me for the reality show *America's Next Top Model*. *Pick me, pick me, pick me* was the circular plea going on inside my head, and I'm pretty sure the girls on either side of me were thinking the same.

My decision to audition for *America's Next Top Model* wasn't exactly well thought-out. In fact, I had only watched a few minutes of the previous cycle before I decided to audition in St. Louis. And, to be honest, my dream in life wasn't necessarily to become a fashion model; it was simply to be valued as a person. I think we all are born with that desire. We all want to be liked and wanted. But instead of looking to faith to help guide me and seeking acceptance and truth from the One who created me, I looked to the world for meaning. And I thought I had found it in Tyra and the TV show.

Standing in that room, waiting for Tyra's selection, and believing I was so close to this very public form of validation was terrifying. What if I ended up getting this close and then didn't get picked? What if, as I stood there hoping, she deemed me unworthy and passed me over? But then she said my name—"Leah Darrow." I couldn't believe it. I tried to play it cool, but she could see that I was totally shocked.

"Surprised?" she asked, as I took my spot with the other Cycle 3 contestants.

"Yeah, a little," I said.

But it was more than just a little. I was a college graduate but still felt completely lost, unsure about who I was and where I was going. I was in that life stage where reality crashes in. During college, I was the star of the undergraduate psychology department, having received every award and graduating magna cum laude. My future had seemed bright. I thought after college I would land an amazing job, have a super cute studio apartment in the city, possibly with a small pet, and spend Saturday afternoons with my girlfriends drinking mimosas on the balcony. I had plans to be somebody. However, the reality was that after college I was working as an assistant manager for Hollister Co., living paycheck to paycheck, balancing student loans and overdue bills, and trying to keep up the act that I had it all together. Not exactly living the dream. My everyday routine made me wonder if all the inspirational messages I'd been told my whole life were true. And then Tyra Banks picked me.

When Tyra Banks called my name, in that moment I believed, subconscious though it might have been, that this meant I was worth more than I had been before. In my mind being chosen for *America's Next Top Model* pointed to the truth that I was wanted, beautiful, and soon-to-be successful. How could it not? I was about to appear on a popular TV show, my modeling career would take off as a result, and, if I won, I'd be valued even more than I could imagine.

But the reality, I discovered, was quite the opposite. Tyra's choice didn't make me happy. And *America's Next Top Model* didn't make me feel wanted, worthy, or beautiful. After all, being eliminated from the show in front of millions of viewers, as I would be a couple of weeks later, can certainly make someone feel unwanted, worthless, and ugly.

But what I've learned since that time is that Tyra wasn't the problem. *America's Next Top Model* wasn't the problem either. The problem was that, for some time in my life, I had accepted imitation beauty and imitation love as the keys to my value and worth. I thought these things were the secret to finding and living a beautiful life.

Starting when I was young, I was brainwashed into believing that my worth was wrapped up in how I looked. After all, from what I had seen in life, beauty seemed to be everything, and love seemed to be given in response to beauty. The more beautiful a thing or person was, the more it was loved. Everywhere I looked, all day and every day, whether it was magazines, social media, television, movies, or advertisements—all the women, no matter what they were doing, looked flawlessly beautiful, from their wardrobe to their hair, nails, apartments, boyfriends, and friends. Even their silly dogs were well groomed. And those who looked beautiful were happy in relationships and had supportive friends.

The hit HBO show *Sex and the City* sucked me in when I was in college and reinforced this worldview. It wasn't difficult to make the connection that beauty and love went hand in hand when the four main women of the show were beautiful, dressed to perfection, always had a handsome date, and survived on cosmopolitans and gossip. Even their bad behavior *looked* beautiful, and so it seemed acceptable, even praiseworthy. Everything about *Sex and the City* revolved around love and beauty, and watching it planted the idea that how I looked was directly related to the quality of my relationships, the love I received from others, and ultimately my worth.

Beyond this fictional television series, though, I also avidly watched *Miss America*, where women annually competed for the title of most beautiful woman in the country. As a little girl I had been mesmerized by the pretty dresses, but as I grew older I found myself judging, along with the crowd, who I thought was more beautiful, walked more gracefully, or looked better in a bikini. From *Miss America* to *Miss Universe*, the message was clear: looking good came down to a panel of judges and ended with a crown. Beauty seemed to go far beyond a single dress or personal care; it was a lifestyle. Without me even knowing it, this culture of beauty warped my mind so that I believed my own worth and value depended on how I looked.

This misunderstanding of beauty and love so deeply affected me that, after being eliminated from *America's Next Top Model*, I decided to move to New York City and pursue a modeling career on my own. If I wasn't going to continue on the show, I was convinced I could still find that worth and happiness on my own.

When I arrived in New York, my picture from *America's Next Top Model* was still on a billboard in Times Square and on the sides of taxicabs and subways, so I had a little leverage and was able to start booking modeling jobs. One of those jobs came from an international magazine. When I sat down with them, they told me they could see I had more to offer than the girl-next-door look; I could be sexy. I was flattered. Here was the proof that I could still do it. Here was the validation that I was worthy, wanted, and beautiful.

But when the day of the photo shoot arrived, something happened that changed my life forever. I encountered true beauty, my heavenly Father, in an unexplainable miraculous moment there on the photo shoot set.

In that moment I started to realize that I didn't need to be famous be to known and loved by God. I didn't need to win *America's Next Top Model* or be put on the cover of a magazine to be deemed beautiful. God didn't want to photoshop me. He saw me with all of my flaws and yet delighted in me. The beauty God had placed within me would not be brought out by lip gloss or concealer, but by kindness, generosity, and joy. And that was a better, deeper, and more lasting beauty than what I had been taught to chase after.

Deep inside I began to sense that God had a different design for my life. I didn't know exactly what it was or how I was going to get there, but I suddenly knew without a doubt that he had a plan for me. And it was better than the way I was currently living. My heart was convinced in that moment that I was made for more; I was made to live out a life for God, not a life lived for myself alone.

The magazine staff was right. I did have more to offer. But it had nothing to do with my body measurements or taking a pretty picture.

I walked out of that photo shoot, never to return again to the modeling world.

Up to that point I had found my worth in the world and its definition of beauty, but it had only led me to despair. It was killing me emotionally, physically, and spiritually. Every photo shoot, every red-carpet event, every date with a new guy, every outfit I put on—all of it had been dependent on how I looked or how my life looked to others. My pursuit for happiness had been based on the exterior. But in doing this, I had neglected the deepest desire of my heart and had abandoned my faith—all because I was afraid God wouldn't really give me the beautiful life I wanted so badly. I feared his path to happiness would be filled with boring days, not-cute guys, and possibly wearing itchy brown-plaid ensembles. No thank you!

But I was mistaken.

I know I'm not the only one who has found herself seduced by imitation beauty. The promise of being and feeling beautiful has been whispered into the ears of millions of girls all over the world. The false promises of the beauty industry have led us to chase after a type of beauty that is unreachable.

In my return to faith and reason, I've gradually come to understand that true beauty should always point to its original source and lead to the development of a beautiful soul. Surprisingly, this has little to do with glitter stilettos or fake eyelashes. Calvin Klein, Chanel, or Dolce & Gabbana do not dictate our worth. God alone does, and he sees us as "very good" (Gen. 1:31).

As I rebuilt my life after *America's Next Top Model* and

walked away from my modeling career, I realized that my worth actually comes from being made, known, and loved by God, and that I am called to a life of love, holiness, and beauty as a result. And that has nothing to do with the imitation beauty the world offers us.

Over the course of this book, together we will uncover the lies the beauty and fashion industry attempt to sell us and the impact these have on our lives as women, not only on how we think about our outward appearances, but also what we believe about our identities, relationships, and roles in the world. More importantly, we will find our way to the truth that we are beautiful, valued, and worthy of love. Not only do these truths change us, but through us, they can change the world.

THE WORLD'S

DEFINITION OF BEAUTY

WHEN YOU HEAR THE WORD *BEAUTY,* WHAT do you think about? For most of my life, my automatic response to that word was to connect it with something exterior, whether that was fashion, clothing size, makeup, physique, hair—you name it. It's not surprising, then, that I often sought out beauty regimes or products that promised—in exchange for my time and money—to make me physically beautiful.

Every product came with the promise of being hand-crafted with me in mind, boasting that it would eliminate my wrinkles, acne, dark circles, muffin top, or varicose veins. Sometimes I didn't even know I had such problems until an advertisement pointed it out to me, and then suddenly it was a glaring issue that I just had to deal with. It sounds pretty foolish now, looking back, but I don't think my former self was alone in thinking about beauty in this way.

This purely physical, perpetually unsatisfied view of beauty is actually rather common. But it shouldn't be. Why? Because the stakes are so high—the way we conceptualize beauty and how we search for it affect not only our outward appearance but how we evaluate our worth, pursue our passions, and, most importantly, how we build our relationships with other people.

Once my eyes were opened, I knew I had to shake off the conceptual hold that the beauty industry had on me; I had to clearly see the truth about this imitation beauty I had been offered. And that truth is that the beauty the industry promises me and you turns its loyal subjects into mere objects. In other words, it objectifies us. I think most women don't realize this as they go about their regular beauty routines, but if they did, they wouldn't want beauty on those terms. Let's explore more about what this objectification means for us.

You Are a Beautiful . . . Hanger

As I mentioned earlier, after I was voted off *America's Next Top Model*, I moved to New York City and went to modeling auditions every week, waiting to get called back, waiting to be validated once again for my look, my beauty, my identity. I was hungry for that feeling I'd had when Tyra had first called my name. In the meantime I bartended at a few bars in

Greenwich Village and became one of New York's finest dog walkers. I also started living with a boyfriend I had met in the city. I was doing everything I had seen portrayed as part of the glamorous life of a young person in New York. And yet it wasn't what I'd imagined it would be.

I still clearly remember one fall afternoon in Bryant Park when the buzz of Fashion Week was everywhere. I had been asked to work for a new designer and walk the runway as part of New York Fashion Week, which is one of the most exciting jobs for a model. I was hoping this would help me move up the fashion ladder.

Passing through security, I looked around and noticed it looked more like a fashion circus than Fashion Week. Models ran around half naked while assistants, stylists, and producers tended to their designers' needs. I found my place, got into hair and makeup, and waited to be called up for my position in the runway show.

And that's when I heard it.

"Get me a new hanger!" a man shouted.

Some assistants ran around, sending texts in a hurry, until a new girl was pushed in front of him.

"Yep, she'll do," he said, and off she went down the runway.

He called us hangers, not women, not models, not humans—hangers. As I stood waiting in line for my time to enter the runway, my turn to be a hanger, I began to think about his comment. *Is that all we are? Just some object, some tool for clothes to be draped over? Is this really my dream, to be a hanger?*

Looking back on this time in my life, I realize that I was merely pretending. I pretended it didn't bother me to be judged by fashion designers and modeling agencies. I pretended to want a life that belonged to someone else's dreams. I pretended to be satisfied with the life I was living, ignoring how empty it actually felt.

You don't have to be a supervillain to be living an unhappy life. Michelangelo, arguably one of the greatest artists and sculptors who ever lived, a man who always strived for excellence in his art, is rumored to have said, "The greatest danger in life to most of us lies not in setting our aim too high and falling short, but in setting our aim too low and achieving the mark." It is so easy to live a life that does not aim for the best version of yourself, to live a life that isn't ultimately beautiful. And that was the life I was living: a life that had a low bar and was mediocre at best.

Not only was I pretending to desire a life that only brought me confusion, but I was also intentionally leaving God out of the equation. What would he have to say about my day-to-day actions? Would he approve of the types of modeling auditions I went on, what I wore, who I dated, or where I lived? I thought of God then only as an obligation for Christians on Sundays for a set amount of time. I did not witness any Christians in my field who spoke openly about the Lord, and I purposely surrounded myself with people who thought and acted the same way I did so that I would not be challenged.

My life at that time had one significant lie at its core: that my body was an object to be used, a means to getting certain ends. I used my body professionally to get further in my career, and I used it personally to feel loved. And I let others use my body, even when I didn't feel like it, so that I could grasp any feeling of value, worth, acceptance, and love.

The problem with being used, whether we allow it to happen or not, is that it does not match up with the dignity God gave us when he created us. And living contrary to our dignity has consequences. We are free to choose anything we want in this world, but we are not free from the consequences of those choices. As the apostle Paul said in 1 Corinthians 10:23, "'All things are lawful,' but not all things are helpful" (ESV). I had followed culture's lie about outward beauty and pursued a career in modeling, seeking identity, worth, acceptance, and love; but instead of gaining those things, I lost my sense of dignity. I allowed myself to be treated like an object, and the consequences of that choice were not what I expected.

On the one hand, willingly using my body for its appearance meant I'd been chosen to be on *America's Next Top Model*. This seemed to reinforce the worldview that good consequences came from using my body. However, soon after I had made it to the top twenty contestants, I was sent home for two weeks to put my affairs in order so that I would be immediately ready to film Cycle 3 in New York should I be selected out of the top twenty. During those two weeks back in St. Louis, friends took me out to bars and clubs and told everyone, "My friend Leah is going to be on TV!" People whom I hadn't spoken to in years suddenly wanted to talk and hang out because there was a chance I'd be on a television show, which gave them bragging rights to say they knew me.

But they didn't care about a real friendship with me, only a friendship of use, as I was about to discover. On one occasion, at a dance club, after my friends basically told the entire bar about my upcoming TV debut, a guy grabbed me and said, "I just want to have my hands on you before you become famous." He proceeded to grope me, putting one hand on my chest and the other on my backside, in front of everyone, until I shoved him off me. I was disgusted and angry at being assaulted like that. This guy thought he had the right to touch me. And, what is possibly worse, my friends didn't jump in to stop him.

While I used my body for personal and professional gains, I was mistaken to think I could control exactly how I wanted to be used. The more I treated myself like an object, the easier it was for others to do so as well. When the consequences got out of control, such as people touching and using me without my consent, I finally realized that I no longer wanted to be treated as if I were just a body. However, the world and that guy at the bar didn't know where I drew the line. That guy assumed that since I put myself on display, he was entitled to use my body as well.

Young girls all over the world strive to be supermodels, all with the idea that the modeling lifestyle will be glamorous, beautiful, and lucrative, giving them a sense of independence and confidence. The reality is that this lifestyle, at its core, steals confidence. It says confidence is on shaky ground since it is dependent on how you look. It creates an atmosphere of dependence on the current cultural standard of beauty, pushing women to do anything and buy anything that helps them look, act, or be a certain way. This only benefits the beauty industry's bottom line—a number that is never large enough—and fuels our consumerism and materialism.

This is not beauty; this is a form of world-class manipulation meant to control how we see ourselves and others. This type of distorted beauty objectifies women and lowers our assessment of our own dignity and value. When we begin to think of ourselves merely as beautiful objects, the world begins to treat us as such. We teach others how to treat us, and if we lower the bar for ourselves, why are we so surprised when the world does the same?

Ironically, although women often allow themselves to be used, women actually don't like seeing themselves portrayed as objects. A study of more than 3,300 women done by the organization Women Not Objects demonstrated that objectifying women in advertising significantly impacted women's buying intent negatively.[1] In other words, we can intuitively pick up that an ad is objectifying a woman, and we generally dislike it. According to this research, an ad objectifies a woman if it (a) treats the woman as a prop or object, (b) retouches the woman's image to the extent that it's beyond anyone's ability to look that way, (c) reduces the woman to a provocative body part, or (d) makes a viewer feel bad thinking a daughter, a friend, or a coworker being portrayed in that manner. The big question seems to be, if the research shows that we women dislike these ads that objectify us, why do we continue to fall for the trap again and again?

I believe the answer has to do with brokenness. If you believe you are broken, you'll accept whatever solution is necessary in order to be fixed. Many of our insecurities come from times when we've been wounded—by past experiences, other people, hurtful words, or the world's suggestions that we need fixing. Whatever the reason, it is easy to live out of those insecurities, and the beauty industry subtly encourages them because the relevance and profitability of their business largely depends on us continuing in our woundedness.

Maybelline, the self-proclaimed "number one cosmetic company in America,"[2] owns the famous tagline "Maybe she's born with it. Maybe it's Maybelline." I grew up with this little jingle branded into my brain, all the while not realizing that it had an effect on me, like so many other beauty advertisements. This jingle has the capability to impress upon women that we couldn't possibly be beautiful on our own, hence the need for this particular cosmetic company's products. Or it could also suggest that if some women who aren't naturally endowed with beauty want to level the playing field, then these cosmetics will help—which only adds fuel to the fire of comparison and competition between women. What a brilliant marketing idea! Impress upon women that we either couldn't possibly be born with beauty or that we should be comparing and competing with others for beauty. This company, like almost every other cosmetics company, wants us to believe that they will be the one to make us beautiful. And in the end, it is not about true beauty at all. It is about exploiting our insecurities or creating new ones so that we believe we need fixing.

Our culture starts this false, self-perpetuating cycle early in a girl's life. It does this by constantly focusing on the exterior and advertising products that claim they will make a girl prettier, from sparkly nail polish and tinted lip balm when she's younger to Spanx and fake eyelashes when she's older. As her insecurities grow, they push her to buy products to address them, thereby funding and empowering the industry, which then puts more money into advertising, and the cycle goes on.

There's nothing inherently wrong with wearing makeup or getting our hair done. But we need to understand that all these things should only serve to enhance the beauty that is already there, not create it. We *are* born with it. Maybe it's time we realized that.

I Promise to Make You Beautiful . . . for at Least a Week

The beauty and fashion industries are built on the back of our insecurities and the notion that a woman's best contribution to the world is how she looks. Without highlighting our physical "flaws" and need to feel beautiful, they would not have the power or influence that they currently have.

In a twisted way, most women are desperate to be hangers. In 2014, we spent more than $56.2 billion on beauty products alone and $250 billion on wearable fashion.[3] In 2015 we spent $15.9 million on cosmetic procedures and around $13.3 billion on elective cosmetic surgeries.[4]

These numbers keep rising every year. How can it be that money on fashion is spent in increasing amounts year after year? Because the beauty industry recreates itself over and over by either pointing out a problem or creating new problems for women. Constantly changing the standard means that women will never be satisfied and will never stop chasing beauty.

According to some, a woman's problems consist in finding the right car or razor made especially for women. Lifestyle and fashion magazine *Cosmopolitan* teamed up with car manufacturer SEAT to create a car just for women. This car debuted during *Cosmo*'s FashFest in London in September 2016. The tiny purple car showcases "'eyeliner shape'" headlights and "jewelled bi-color rim design" on the wheels that add a "surprise sparkle,"[5] and according to *Cosmopolitan*, is a "place for impromptu karaoke performances, last-minute wardrobe changes, dramatic gossip sessions and emergency lunch-hour kips."[6] The message that this car sends is that beautiful women wear eyeliner, love jewels and sparkles, and spend their time doing karaoke, changing clothes, and gossiping. Thus, every woman should buy this car, even if you find another perfectly functional car. But what if you don't wear eyeliner or love jewels and sparkles? What if you only have a few outfits and don't enjoy karaoke? The subtle message is that you aren't a real woman. But why are those the standards of what makes a woman? Do we really need a car just for women? What problem does this car solve that other cars can't? These sorts of products and marketing strategies take advantage of women and subtly suggest how we should define ourselves and what we should base our own value on.

From big things to small, it seems there is no shame in taking advantage of women. Razors are another example of a beauty standard we women did not create but have allowed to shape our lives. The practice of shaving for Western women is a relatively new development. While we can find evidence of Egyptian and Roman women shaving sections of body hair in an effort to denote wealth and class, most women in history did not shave due to the harsh effects of shaving with pumice stones or sharp rocks. Shaving for women was not introduced into Western society until the early 1900s when images of women wearing sleeveless and short dresses in print magazines began to change the culture. In 1915 the magazine *Harper's Bazaar* featured a woman wearing a sleeveless summer dress with one arm raised, showcasing a hairless armpit. The ad appealed to women's vanity with this line: "Summer dress and modern dancing combine to make necessary the removal of objectionable hair."[7] The suggestion is that if you want to be a modern woman who wears summer dresses and goes dancing, who is desirable and beautiful, you'd better shave those pits. And now the vast majority of Western women do just that.

As much as we may sigh at the women reading *Harper's Bazaar* in 1915, we're all guilty of chasing after the newest and latest fashion trends. But ask yourself, if you have a fundamental desire for something, whether it be to fix a flaw or to enjoy something good, don't you want to satisfy that desire once and for all? If I have a desire for a friend, don't I want a friend who will be there for me forever? If I have a desire to be beautiful, don't I want my beauty to last? What good is the cream I bought today if I have to rebuy it in a few months? If we spend this obscene amount of money year after year, then the products are obviously not producing lasting effects and are not filling the void.

You might respond, "Come on, Leah. You're too intense. Beauty products aren't like friends; they're like food. You need to eat food every day, which is why it is fun to try new recipes and buy new food. Isn't fashion and beauty more like food than like something that is long-lasting like a friend?"

But I would say beauty is absolutely more like a friend than like food! It is not temporary. Your beauty will be with you until the day you die and beyond into the next life. If you build up your beauty like you build up your friends, it will not leave you.

The main reason we have this idea that beauty is temporary is because we think beauty is merely physical. And physical things are temporary. Food spoils over time, flowers wither, and our skin dries and wrinkles. Aging is now considered a disease we must fight. During one of the audition rounds for *America's Next Top Model*, one of the judges on the panel was clearly concerned about my age. I was twenty-three at the time. This judge told me that I *might* have a few years left—if I was lucky. A few years? Was aging a death sentence? Was my life's potential over before it had even begun?

In the beauty industry, youth is king, and that means that there's only a small window of time in our lives when we possess what the world considers most valuable. And so we spend lots of money (another physical thing) to try to maintain our short-lived physical beauty. We even go to great lengths to pretend we are younger than we are. Surgeries, lifts, injectables—we will do whatever it takes to look younger because we, at some level, acknowledge the lie that our worth and sense of beauty derive from the physical.

Somehow our world has become an international beauty pageant, and we're all contestants whether we like it or not. Everywhere we look, we find people comparing themselves to one another, rating others based on their looks, assigning value to some while others are quickly discarded. And even if you're on top one day, that's no guarantee you'll be there the next. When everything is physical and everything is constantly in motion, then your status and your value are always at risk. Your beauty can't escape being merely temporary. This is no way to live, at least not happily.

Every Girl Can Be Beautiful . . . for a Price

If beauty is merely physical and temporary, it is also buyable. And if it is buyable, then it is only for those who can afford it. Beauty, in the eyes of our world, is a wealthy person's luxury and a poor person's envy. From makeup and fashion to cosmetic surgery, beauty has been peddled to us as something we need to be an in-style, complete woman and as something we can obtain, as long as we are willing to pay. And do we ever pay for it.

In Brazil, cosmetic surgery is seen as an "investment." Women from the wealthiest to the poorest save money for surgeries, so it's not surprising that Brazil has just passed the United States as the country with the largest number of cosmetic surgeries. The way we portray ourselves does matter, without a doubt, but Western culture has elevated the exterior to an extreme that is hazardous and incomplete. One Brazilian woman, after her sixth cosmetic surgery, said, "There's nothing better than getting a compliment, right? That you're good, that you're sexy, it's really good. I like it."[8] Our culture's focus on what we look like has become the standard by which we measure not just beauty, but worth. If you look good, you are good.

While you might be tempted to dismiss Brazil as an outlier or as operating under a culture fundamentally different from American culture, don't be so hasty. It is we in the United States who create the competition around the world for buyable beauty. What is happening in Brazil is just the downstream effect of us blindly chasing imitation beauty.

Companies take advantage of our desire to meet a certain standard of beauty. Coincidentally and conveniently, when *Harper's Bazaar* first released ads encouraging hairless armpits and legs, Gillette released their first razor for women. But razor companies didn't just make a small profit off the existence of the new beauty trend; they profited exorbitantly.

Razor companies doubled and even tripled the prices for women's razors compared to men's razors. Does a pink handle, a moisturizing bar that only lasts two shaves, a light or a vibrating handle really make a difference in shaving? To expose this nonsensical price gouging, the company Dollar Shave Club emerged to bring levity and common sense to the matter. They provide razors for as little as three dollars a month. Compare that to what you pay for razors the next time you're at the store.

Razors aren't the only items getting a price hike just because they are made for women. In 2012 talk-show host Ellen DeGeneres used her platform and humor to talk about "lady pens."[9] Bic produced a line of pens made especially for women, titled "Bic for Her." The package explained the pink and purple pens were "beautifully smooth" and "designed to fit a woman's hand." But beyond the girly colors and supposedly perfect fit, these pens were also priced three times higher than other retractable pens made by Bic. Along the same lines, according to a 2015 study by the New York City Department of Consumer Affairs, shampoo and conditioner marketed to women cost an average of 48 percent more than those marketed to men,[10] women's jeans cost 10 percent more than men's,[11] and girls' bikes and scooters cost 6 percent more than boys'.[12] Overall, the study found that products marketed to women cost more 42 percent of the time.[13] Being a woman should not entail a product tax.

What's even more tragic about this commodification, though, is that we spend more on beauty products, fashion, and cosmetic surgeries than we do on helping others. In 2015, we spent more than $306 billion on fashion. Compare that to the amount of money Americans donated as individuals to nonprofit organizations in 2015: a little more than $264 billion.[14] We spent $42 billion more on how we look than on helping others. In a recent survey in the documentary *Chasing Beauty*, more than 25 percent of young American women said that they would rather win *America's Next Top Model* than the Nobel Peace Prize. Further, more than 23 percent of young American women would rather lose the ability to read than lose their figures.[15]

What does it say about our women and about our culture if we'd rather look good than do good? So many young women today have swallowed the same lie I did about what beauty is. We look to the world for answers, for help, for validation, and to be told we are good, beautiful, and worthy. But instead, we develop a sense of inadequacy that we believe can only be cured by a product, a look, or a lifestyle. Is this you? It sure was me, and, to be honest, it's still something I catch myself struggling with sometimes.

But here's what I've learned along the way: when we allow our desires to be dictated by the beauty industry's ideology, we begin to navigate our lives by *their* desires and *their* goals, which are primarily to entrap us into believing that we need them—we need to look like that, we need a guy like that, we need a loft/apartment/house like that, we need, we need, we need.

What we really need is a reality check. We need to be

reminded, "The world doesn't need what women have; it needs what women are." These are the words of Edith Stein, a woman who lived through World War I and died in a Nazi concentration camp in World War II. A nurse, a philosopher, and later a nun, she saw firsthand the evil that bad ideologies can do to the world. To be a woman is to be more than our parts. It is to be more than the length of our lashes or the plumpness and color of our lips.

The more we define beauty as merely temporary, physical, and buyable, the more we fall into the trap and, worse yet, the more we neglect and abandon the beauty that really matters, the beauty that God values. Beauty in kindness, gratitude, and forgiveness. Beauty in reaching out to and loving those who need help, who are lonely, and who are forgotten.

Strange how something as simple as beauty can have such an impact on our lives, deeper than we might imagine. I was searching for beauty because I believed that beauty would save me. I believed that beauty just might give me everything I ever wanted.

I wasn't wrong. But I was after the wrong kind of beauty.

THE HIGH COST OF

IMITATION BEAUTY

I HAD BEEN PLUCKING AND SHAPING MY EYE-brows since high school, and whenever I had a little extra cash, I'd treat myself to an eyebrow wax at the spa. But, one time, in an effort to save a few bucks, I purchased an at-home eyebrow-wax kit. You know the kind. They promise a smooth, pain-free experience, all-natural ingredients, and perfectly shaped eyebrows. I climbed up and sat atop the bathroom counter to get a better view. I read the instructions, whipped out that green wax, and applied away.

My right eyebrow went great, and it actually wasn't that painful. So far I was really liking my new beauty product. Trying to be environmentally frugal, I decided to reuse one of the waxing cloths for my left eyebrow, since it still had a large unused portion of wax-free cloth. As I waxed the arch of my eyebrow and ripped the cloth away, I screamed bloody murder.

My husband, Ricky, came flying up the stairs. "Are you okay? What's wrong with your eye?"

I was scrying—the combination of screaming and crying—while covering my left eyebrow. Ricky pulled my hand away, and I knew with one look that it was bad, really bad. He flinched. I turned toward the mirror and, with a dropped jaw, gawked at my *two* left eyebrows. Somehow the old wax on the cloth from my right eyebrow had clung to the center of my left eyebrow, and off it went. There was now a huge, smooth, hairless gap smack-dab in the middle of my left eyebrow.

We're all so careful not to have a unibrow, but now I had not one, not two, but three eyebrows. I tried using an eyebrow pencil to fill in the gap, but it just ended up looking like a toddler's artwork. It took months for the hair to regrow and called for a whole lot of humility on my part. This was the cost I paid for beauty.

We all have stories like this, stories of doing something in the name of beauty, even if it results in pain, blisters, or waxing blunders. Many of us have been told, "It hurts to be beautiful" or "You have to suffer for beauty," but where do we draw the line? What cost is too high? The desire to be and feel beautiful can lead to us actually hurting ourselves, and blisters from a pair of high heels are the least of the costs.

Body for Sale

As we talk about the costs of following and pursuing the world's definition of beauty, we have to start at the root of so many of the costs: the way we accept an overall sense of diminished value for ourselves. We can see this not only in our choices about what to wear or what makeup to use but in the lifestyle that results: the way the world's lies about beauty, identity, and worth bleed into our relationships, our self-esteem, our mental health, and our connection to others.

While I was modeling in New York City, I made the decision to move in with my boyfriend, Ryan. We lived in a cute, crazy-small apartment in the Lower East Side of Manhattan. Even though we shared an apartment, were intimate, and "loved" each other, it was clear early on that marriage was off the table. He told me he just wasn't ready for that. We shared in all the benefits of marriage, except for the "I'm going to love you and stay with you forever" part.

I acted as though having merely temporary value to my boyfriend didn't bother me. After all, if I believed I was defined by my outward appearance—physical, temporary, buyable—it only made sense that "real-life" and "grown-up" relationships were the same way. I even pretended I wanted a no-strings-attached relationship. Not wanting to sound cliché or needy, I acted as if I was totally fine with sacrificing my life, body, and time on the off chance that one day he *might* decide to be with me forever and make it official with a marriage proposal.

Our relationship was conditional. It was about as stable as our rent in New York City. And, in fact, that is exactly the phrase I heard from a guy at a bar after I'd moved to New York. He was talking about his live-in girlfriend, and he said, "I'm renting with the option to buy." I was taken aback. He was talking about his girlfriend! When did we women become like real estate? I was shocked and disgusted to hear this guy talk about his girl this way, but then I realized I was in that same boat.

Ryan wasn't crass enough to say it, but we were essentially living it. Our love was conditional, and our relationship was like an apartment lease. It had a time limit on it. And, sure enough, when our lease was up, so was our love. Ryan and I ended our relationship, and off we went, each going our separate ways. The leased love had the final say.

Cohabitation may seem harmless enough on the surface of things. Two people who care about each other want to spend time together, so they move in together. They make the decision to have sex, enjoying each other's bodies and outward beauty. *It's no big deal*, they tell themselves. *It's just a physical thing, not anything deeper.* So they give themselves to each other, but then, when the question comes up about possibly making a commitment greater than an apartment lease, it seems to be a step further than most Americans want to take. We want relationships that look like marriage but without the official commitment, just something temporary that doesn't tie us down too much.

It is perhaps ironic, then, that this temporary commitment—this attempt to avoid making things permanent—results in added pressure to stay together, even if the couple has doubts, because the stakes are higher now and there is more to lose. It literally involves the roof over their heads, a lease, money, shared utilities, furniture, and even the communal pet. They end up staying in the relationship because it is convenient to have a roommate pay half the rent. And then, suddenly, they have become buyable.

Often we think that living with our significant other will help us make a more informed decision about a longer type of commitment, namely marriage, but outside of having shared living quarters, it does not truly resemble what a happy marriage is supposed to look like. Ideally, marriage is a public, permanent commitment established before God between two people who, through thick and thin, choose to work it out. In fact, let's take a look at the implications of the traditional marriage vows.

> I take you for my lawful wife/husband, to have and to hold from this day forward, for better, for worse, for richer, for poorer, in sickness and health, until death do us part.

Marriage is designed to be forever, not just temporary, and it is meant to hold true in both good times and bad. It is for rich and poor alike—it cannot be bought—and it continues in health and in sickness, going beyond the physical. So you see, at its core, marriage is the polar opposite of temporary, buyable, and physical. Marriage treats each person in the relationship with the value, dignity, and worth that God has given to every man and woman he lovingly created.

Cohabitation, on the other hand, has its own vows that go more like this:

> I take you to be my cohabitant. To have sex with you and to hold you responsible for half the bills. To love and to take advantage of you from this day forward or for as long as our arrangement works out. I will be more or less faithful to you as long as my needs are met and if nothing better comes along. If we should break up, it does not mean this wasn't special to me because I love you almost as much as I love myself. I commit to live with you as long as it works out. So help me—me.[1]

While cohabitation may be seen by many as an alternative or prelude to marriage, current research tells us that if a long-term commitment is the end goal, cohabitation will be a wrong turn down Lovers' Lane.[2]

It is clear to me now that when I chose that unhealthy relationship during my time in New York, I ended up being treated like an object, not a person. While I thought I was in love and believed that he was the "one" for me, I ended up having to face some hard facts. I was expendable if I wasn't being useful (paying the bills) and if I didn't provide physical pleasure (regular sex). Trust me, I did not want to admit this to myself. Ryan was funny, kind, and thoughtful. But we clearly shared a definition of love that was based on how useful the other person was. No one likes to admit difficult truths, especially when it comes to love. But I finally realized that this relationship was based on what I could usefully offer and what external value I brought to the table, and that was something that could not last for too long.

Sure enough, my idea of love, beauty, and life soon started falling apart. Living in New York City, pursuing a modeling career after my time on *America's Next Top Model*, and moving in with my boyfriend should have put me in beauty and love mecca. But I didn't feel beautiful and loved. Instead, I felt suffocated. My continual search for love, taking advice from peers and *Cosmopolitan*, landed me in dead-end relationships, and my search for beauty in front of the camera led me to a destructive body image, vanity, and ultimately self-hate. I literally felt like I was drowning in this world where what I offered was never good enough.

Anxiety, low self-esteem, distorted body image, and depression—these among others were what I discovered to be the natural consequences of chasing after imitation beauty and accepting my subsequent objectification. I thought beauty would be liberating, but instead I became a slave to its power, a minion in the world of distorted beauty that steals our joy, our courage, and our sense of worth.

But the truth that I did not understand at the time was that God did not make our bodies for public consumption or consumerism. We are not the sum of our physical attributes and what we can contribute to others' satisfaction. All those thoughts about how we are not good enough, skinny enough, or perfect enough are, quite plainly, lies.

Let me tell you the truth: You are enough. You are more

than enough. God made you, and God does not make junk. "For you created my inmost being; you knit me together in my mother's womb" (Ps. 139:13 NIV). You are not just a body; you are a body and a soul. You have an inmost being that does not come from your parents, from the physical DNA that they gave you, but from God Almighty who breathed life specially and intentionally into your very self. Not only did God create you, he continues to watch over you and care for you. "Indeed, the very hairs of your head are all numbered. Don't be afraid" (Luke 12:7 NIV).

You are more than your makeup, the number on the scale, or the designer of your clothes. You are more than your thick or thin hair, your skin color, and the shape of your lips or eyebrows. You were not made to fit into some kind of beauty or fashion mold. You were made for more. Pope Francis said, "Things have a price and can be for sale, but people have a dignity that is priceless and worth far more than things."[3] He was saying what a long line of Christians have said. The Bible clearly tells us our worth is based on far more than what others can see on the outside, but when we buy into the culture's imitation beauty and the objectification and diminished worth that follow, the cost is enormous. In fact, it goes way beyond our internal mind-sets and how we think about ourselves; it can even harm our very bodies.

Physical Health

Did you know that striving for beauty can be physically dangerous? A study conducted in 2007 revealed that of the thirty-three top lipsticks, 60 percent contained lead, a known neurotoxin, as well as several other metals, such as titanium and aluminum, also known neurotoxins. Not only did they test for the existence of toxic elements, but the study also estimated "potential daily intakes." In other words, how much lipstick are you likely to lick and absorb in a day? They demonstrated that by their estimates, a woman would absorb several of the metals above at a level beyond the acceptable daily intake recommended by the FDA. As Bill Chameides, the dean of Duke University's Nicholas School of the Environment, so aptly said in his *Huffington Post* article, "I suggest a sign be posted at the lipstick counter: 'Use At Your Own Risk—Don't Lick Your Lips.'"[4]

Do you ever look at what ingredients are in the beauty products you use on a daily basis? Most of us don't. Would it shock you to learn that more than 1,300 toxic ingredients used in beauty products are banned in Europe while only eleven are banned in the United States?[5] The last time the FDA updated its guidelines on regulating cosmetics and personal care products was in 1938.[6] That was before my mother was born. A lot has changed since then! We know so much more about health and what's safe to use now, but for some reason we're behind the curve on regulating these ingredients. This is an urgent issue, since, on average, Americans use anywhere between six to twelve products a day. I'm not saying we should all throw away our makeup, but we should be proactive about knowing what is in the products we regularly use!

A good place to start is to look into The Never List,

compiled by a company called Beautycounter. This list identifies questionable or harmful chemical ingredients that should be avoided at all costs (see appendix A). Set aside some time to gather all your products and see if any of them contain these chemicals. If they do, throw them out and find some safer alternatives! It may seem like a hassle right now, but I guarantee it's worth it in the long run.

Another way our preoccupation with physical beauty hurts our bodies is through the myriad strategies we employ to try to lose weight. While some beauty products that look good on the outside have a toxic center, others' ugliness isn't even hidden. According to a study from the National Women's Health Information Center, 13 percent of women elect to smoke in the hopes of losing weight.[7] Even though we know that smoking is unhealthy, we choose a beauty standard over knowledge.

In a fact sheet from the American Lung Association, we see that "women have been extensively targeted in tobacco marketing dominated by themes of an association between social desirability, independence, weight control and smoking messages conveyed through advertisements featuring slim, attractive, and athletic models."[8] The ALA has also admitted that "teenage girls often start to smoke to avoid weight gain and to identify themselves as independent and glamorous, which reflect images projected by tobacco ads. Social images can convince teens that being slightly overweight is worse than smoking. Cigarette advertising portrays cigarettes as causing slimness and implies that cigarette smoking suppresses appetite."[9]

I was one of those girls who fell for this ad campaign, and it cost me dearly. I started smoking in college. At first it was because the group I was hanging out with smoked, and their smoke breaks seemed like bonding moments I was missing out on. So I took up smoking to feel like I was part of the group. Plus, I had heard smoking reduced your appetite and kept you thin, so it was a win-win for me. I ignored the health warnings in the hopes of joining a social group and out of the desire to be skinny.

After ten years of smoking, though, I woke up one morning coughing and unable to take a deep breath. That scared me, and I knew exactly what was to blame. Before even leaving the bed, I vowed never to smoke again. I wanted to be able to take a breath of fresh air, to exercise or run up a flight of stairs without coughing. In the end, smoking did not foster a better social tier for me, nor did it make me skinnier. But it did increase my risk for lung cancer.

Companies and infomercials target weight loss for a reason. Approximately 91 percent of women are unhappy with their bodies, and so they resort to dieting to achieve their ideal body shape.[10] I have tried some ridiculous fad diets in my time. The craziest was when I went an entire month drinking only hot water spiked with lemon juice, cayenne pepper, and maple syrup, commonly called the Master Cleanse. It has been around since the 1970s but gained momentum when Beyoncé Knowles-Carter did it for her role in the movie *Dreamgirls*. I remember reading in a celebrity-gossip magazine that she lost twenty pounds in ten days with the detox cleanse for the movie. Since I was always striving for perfection and looking for quick and easy ways to lose those pesky five or ten pounds, I tried it. I felt terrible and, obviously, very hungry because I was starving myself. At the end of the thirty days, I did lose weight, but I felt physically weak and fatigued, and I lacked mental clarity. Definitely not what I was going for.

While detox diets claim to perform a detoxification of one's gut, which is necessary due to the increase in toxins found in food and the environment, these fads are really aimed at weight loss. The detox theory states that toxins accumulate in one's body, causing headaches, acne, chronic illness, fatigue, and the list goes on, but current medical research does not support this claim. Peter Pressman, internal medicine specialist at Cedars-Sinai Medical Center in Los Angeles, reports, "The science behind the detox theory is deeply flawed."[11] The human body already has multiple systems in place that do a perfectly good job of eliminating toxins from the body. A healthy lifestyle of simply maintaining a balanced diet and avoiding large quantities of junk food, caffeine, and alcohol go a long way toward eliminating fatigue, headaches, and skin-care concerns while not putting your body at risk.[12]

It's clear that our blanket acceptance of imitation beauty is ultimately harmful to our bodies—and even deadly in some cases. You'd think that, at least in terms of our bodily health, we'd take care of ourselves a bit better if we bought into the world's concept that beauty is limited to the physical realm. Unfortunately, reality shows this is not the case, and these high costs of beauty profoundly affect our physical health and life—and our mental and emotional health as well.

Mental Health

The root of the physical costs we've been exploring ultimately comes back to the lies we've bought into and the mind-sets that result from following them. Advertising tells us we should feel bad about ourselves in more ways than we can count. Rather than embrace the differences of each stage of a woman's life, we oversexualize young girls, encouraging them to look older and sexier, while older women try to regain a more youthful and innocent look. In fact, you might be surprised to find out that some of the "women" modeling adult women's fashions on the runway aren't even old enough to get their first period.

Confusion over who we are supposed to be or look like sadly takes a toll on our mental health in a variety of ways. A poor body image is closely linked to low self-esteem, and low self-esteem in adolescents can lead to early sexual activity, substance use, and eating disorders.[13] Eating disorders have the highest mortality rate of any mental illness and affect all races and ethnic groups. Eating disorders can also affect a person at any age. Improbable as it may seem, 42 percent of first- to third-grade girls want to be thinner.[14] That is, little girls between the ages of six and eight who haven't even mastered advanced multiplication and division are already aware of and affected by unhealthy body and beauty standards! The percentage practically doubles by the time girls are ten years old, with 81 percent afraid of being fat.[15] This hyperawareness of body image easily leads to unhealthy behaviors.

The National Association of Anorexia Nervosa and Associated Disorders have reported that nearly 70 percent of girls in grades five through twelve said magazine images influence their ideals of a perfect body.[16] Many factors, such as media exposure and family dynamics, go into the why behind these statistics and subsequent illnesses. Beauty and fashion industries are not the primary cause of eating disorders, but they do contribute to unhealthy and unrealistic body and beauty ideals.

I saw this personally when I was in high school. I was the new girl when Kourtney[17] befriended me. Early in our friendship, she confided that she had been diagnosed with anorexia before she graduated eighth grade. This was the first time I had been face-to-face with a person who suffered from anorexia. Her stories about anorexia made it sound both dangerous and exciting. Even though Kourtney was in treatment, she didn't always follow the protocol, and it was clear she still struggled in accepting therapy and help. During lunch she would tell me what she had eaten or not eaten the night before and what she had planned for the current day's meals. It became obvious that food, exercise, and her weight consumed every thought.

Since she was thin, everyone already assumed she had a problem, which didn't help her self-consciousness, so in the beginning of our sophomore year, I restricted my diet to match hers in an effort to help her not feel bad or alone. But after a few weeks I couldn't keep up with matching her small lunch snacks; I was starving. As an athlete, my lifestyle needed more than a few carrots, a cheese wedge, and a shared slice of turkey.

Kourtney never wanted an eating disorder; she just wanted to lose a couple of pounds. But any compliment Kourtney received, whether on her appearance, grades, or attitude, she attributed to being skinny and losing weight. As she set weight-loss goals and achieved them, a sense of euphoria came over her, and it became obvious that she began to crave those highs. The attention, coupled with her sense of self-satisfaction, became a dangerous game she would play for the next ten years.

I remember hanging out in her room before Friday night football games, and she would say, "Am I a ten?" I didn't understand the question, and she said, "You know, a ten is perfect. Ten out of ten is always my goal." Looking good wasn't enough for Kourtney; she wanted perfection more than anything. We would spend hours on the weekends together looking through celebrity and fashion magazines to find the perfect model figure for our new goal.

After high school we went to different colleges in Missouri. In April of my junior year, my mom called and told me the news that Kourtney had attempted suicide and was in the hospital for treatment. I couldn't believe it. Weeks later I went to visit her, and all I could utter was "What happened, Kourtney?"

She told me that her anorexia had grown worse in college, and although she had been receiving treatment and therapy, she slowly began to ignore the advice and treatment from her psychiatrist, nutritionist, and medical doctors. After months of diving deep into the darkness of anorexia, Kourtney was literally wasting away at a whopping ninety pounds on her five-foot-eight frame. During that hospital visit, we spoke about our days in high school together. I apologized for joining in on her "diet" and also for not speaking up about her health.

Before I left she told me, "I have been listening to this dark voice inside of me, the voice of my eating disorder, that constantly tells me I am not good enough, smart enough, or thin enough. I need to find beauty again, in myself and in the world." After that experience, Kourtney, thank God, chose to receive medical attention, and the long road to recovery began for her.

The beauty and fashion industry marketers are selling an illusion that, like it did to Kourtney, will destroy your self-esteem and ultimately brainwash you into believing that you need them in order to be beautiful. However, the solution isn't to buy more products. In fact, the most common and effective type of therapy for eating disorders and body-image issues is cognitive behavior therapy, a type of therapy whose goal is to change patterns of thinking or behavior that are behind people's difficulties, in order to change the way they feel.[18] This type of therapy, sometimes combined with medication, is very effective because the root of eating and body-image disorders is a warped sense of self, something developed over years of taking in a certain kind of image and the message that comes with it.

These images of physical perfection are everywhere. They

are in children's books and embodied in dolls like Bratz and Barbie. They are shown nonstop in commercials and television shows. "One of the major underlying causes for increasing low self-esteem among young people is that they do not see their uniqueness reflected back at them within the media environment that surrounds them," says leading UK psychotherapist Dr. Susie Orbach. "They see so many perfected images of girls and women that this idea of how they need to be seeps into them, leading them to feel their own loveliness is inadequate."[19] Studies such as *Body Image: An Introduction to Advertising and Body Image* show that looking at magazines for just sixty minutes lowers the self-esteem of more than 80 percent of girls.[20] And when you consider that the body fat of models and actresses portrayed in the media is at least half that of healthy women, it isn't surprising that six out of ten teenage girls think they'd "be happier if they were thinner."[21]

Our mental health is constantly undermined by the fashion and beauty industry, as it holds up a false, unattainable ideal that can drive us to despair. And the thing is, we're not meant to attain it, because if we did, the beauty industry would lose customers. So the ideal must always be out of reach, which ultimately, for all our purchasing power and efforts, leaves us grasping in the air.

Fast Fashion

Not only does the fashion industry negatively impact each one of us individually and personally, but it has global ramifications, especially for women, affecting their very lives.

A recent cause has been popping up in the fashion industry, a call to arms for "ethical fashion." On the surface this cause may simply seem to be a push for "Made in the USA" products, but at its heart, this is not a cause only about American jobs and products. Ethical fashion is about ethical treatment, pay, and safe environments for those who are literally making the products we buy and throw away every day.

The big fashion houses don't want us to dig further into this. They want us to be more concerned about saving money and buying the newest trend at a fraction of the cost, rather than wondering about who made the clothes and under what circumstances.

But the problem goes back a long way to when fashion houses would only turn out four fashion seasons: fall, winter, spring, summer. Whenever designers used to put their fashions on the runway, other second-, third-, and fourth-tier fashion warehouses would replicate this fashion to put in their stores so that someone who could not afford a $487 shirt on the runway could afford the same type of shirt made for a department store for $45.

The problem now is that new fashion trends are introduced far more frequently. Instead of four fashion seasons, there are fifty-two seasons—every week is its own season. And these new fashion trends that are being pushed to the consumer every seven days are cheap. Very cheap. This allows the customer to spend more in an attempt to keep up with what's "in," even though it will be "out" in a week. Boutiques and clothing department stores cannot keep up with the demand of fifty-two weeks of new fashion—and this is where the concept of fast fashion was born.

Fast fashion is the ability to send off new designs and have them made in record time. They are made cheaply and sold cheaply. However, the people making these "great buys" for us are treated just as cheaply. The makers of fast fashion are in third world countries where men and women (but mostly women) are treated like cattle with poor working conditions and are paid less than four dollars a day. Women are pressured into having abortions just to keep their jobs, and they often send away whatever kids they do have to be raised by relatives because their clothing factory jobs mean at least twelve-hour days almost every single day.[22]

Not only are the working conditions harsh, they can be deadly. On April 24, 2013, one of these fast-fashion garment factories in Bangladesh, India, collapsed, killing 1,134 people who were crushed and trapped by the rubble. The day before the collapse, an engineer had examined the building and deemed it unsafe. Yet, in the name of the almighty dollar, the owner forced his employees to return to work the next day.[23] This factory is just one drop in the bucket. There are more than five thousand garment factories in Bangladesh alone.[24]

Ever wonder how stores can produce the newest, trendiest outfit just days after a celebrity wore it? Fast fashion.

H&M is the poster child for fast fashion. Walk into one of their fashion megastores, and you won't recognize or find what you saw the week before. Here, fashion moves at the speed of greed. They've even pushed a line called Conscious Collection with celebrity spokespeople such as Olivia Wilde. But why have a "conscious collection" when your regular collection treats people so unconscionably?

The beauty and fashion industries want us to become so busy with trying to keep up with the latest trend that we forget to ask if we should be consuming so much and at what cost. Would you buy a cheap shirt knowing that it cost someone their hand? Or even their life? I hope not. We can aid others around the world when we bypass fast fashion. When we don't really need to buy a new outfit, we should seriously consider practicing self-control and step back from the mindset of needing a new closetful of clothes every week.

I don't know about you, but I don't need more clothes. I need more peace. And sadly, I can't find that at the mall or on Amazon. We live in a world that is all about excess and the temporary pleasure we get from replacing the new with the latest. From our phones to our clothes, everything is good enough until the next version comes out. Then it's out with the old and in with the new. The spirit of materialism constantly nags at us, trying to make us believe we need more to be happy. And, sadly, we get more at others' expense.

A few years ago, as an antidote to the consumerist spirit of our culture, I did the Closet Challenge for the first time. This was an idea that my friend Sarah Kroger and I came up with, where we wore only seven items of clothing for thirty days. While it sounds restrictive, it was actually liberating. The fundamental goal of the Closet Challenge was to instill gratitude for what we already have and to help us learn to live with less. By eliminating the abundance of our clothing options, we hoped to have more time to prayerfully reflect on how God has blessed us *and* be more grateful for all the blessings already in our lives. Let me tell you, it was an amazing, eye-opening time. I strongly encourage you to try it. (For more details on the Closet Challenge, see appendix C.)

We're all searching for value, for love, for beauty. While there is nothing wrong with looking good, we've sadly elevated it to a height that is unreachable, even by us. And yet we keep trying, fueled by comparison and competition. We see others as our competition instead of as our sisters in Christ. And so we forget who we are and that we are all in this struggle together. This is the highest cost of imitation beauty: the loss of both who God made us to be and the community he designed for our good—and ultimately for the good of the world.

3

FALSE LOVE AND THE

PURSUIT OF WORTH

A LOT OF TIMES OUR DESIRES ARE WARPED BY our wounds. In my case, I deeply wanted to be told I was beautiful, which is a good desire in and of itself. Unfortunately, my desire had been twisted by the wounds I carried around in my heart, and these painful places also made me susceptible to the world's messages about beauty. I can see clearly now that all along my real desire was to be valued and loved for who I am. And so, as I chased after beauty, what I had subconsciously hoped to gain—worth and love—was actually impossible to attain because I had ultimately misunderstood what authentic love was.

My story is the story of thousands of other girls out there. And I know this because they have told me. I speak to tens of thousands of girls a year, and between the conversations I have with them afterward and the emails that fill my inbox days later, I can tell you that I am not alone. This is why I am sharing my heart and, in particular, this story with you—to let you know that you are not alone.

I was the new girl. My family had just moved from Oklahoma to Missouri, and I found myself not knowing a single soul in my new high school at the start of my sophomore year. I wanted friends and hoped I would find my "group" soon so I wouldn't have to continue eating my lunch in a bathroom stall. Moving to a new city often makes a person feel vulnerable because the people who once valued and loved them are no longer present. As human beings, we are made to be social creatures. We want to be loved, so we do things that we think will make people love us. But the question is, what do these people we're trying to impress consider "love" to be, and what counts as lovable in their eyes?

As I was trying to figure this out for myself in this new situation, I noticed a lot of girls had boyfriends. And the ones who didn't have boyfriends were boy crazy—not that I wasn't, but boys had never consumed my every thought up until that point. It seemed obvious that boys were a way I could connect: I'd have something to talk about with other girls, and maybe then I'd find a group to hang with. When the first boy came along who showed interest, I clung to him. I liked the attention; it made me feel special, singled out, and wanted. I wanted someone to want me, but I never questioned if I wanted him.

I don't remember even asking myself if I liked this boyfriend. I never questioned if this person was good for me—whether he came from a good family, dealt drugs, was flunking out of school, or liked movies. I didn't even wonder anything as simple as what his favorite candy bar was. All I knew was that he played soccer, was a senior, and liked me. I was blinded by the possibility of love and was using this poor boy to fill up my desire to be loved and valued.

Not only did I desire to be loved by my boyfriend, but I desired to be loved by others for the fact that I *had* a boyfriend. Having a boyfriend was a status symbol, a way of appearing beautiful and desirable.

Surprisingly I was more aware of and concerned with my appearance when my status went from "single" to "girlfriend." I suddenly felt like I had to look good or he might lose interest and break up with me. Prior to having a boyfriend, a typical Friday night for me involved a football game and maybe a bonfire get-together with friends afterward. I would not have worried all that much about my clothes, my hair, or my makeup. I still would have cared enough to look nice, but I'd have been more concerned with staying warm than with prancing around in a cute outfit. Now that I had a boyfriend, I suddenly felt more pressure. To me, being a girlfriend implied that I had a duty to look good all the time. If I was taken, I had to prove to others I was worthy of the status. This, I told myself, was the cost of being loved.

Most of us long for the experience of being loved before we even know what love is. We just want the feeling, and our hope is that maybe the feeling of love will ultimately teach us what love itself is. If life were void of lies, betrayal, pain, and sin, that method just might work. But life is a battleground where truth wars against lies and good against evil, so the truth about love and worth is easily lost in the struggle.

We use the word *love* so often these days that its meaning and importance are watered down. We love pizza, shoes, lipstick, people, TV shows, and much more. We love using the word *love* so much that it has become an acceptable form of approval for anything or anyone. As long as it's a shade above repulsive, we love it.

But love deserves more than that. Authentic love, love rooted in truth, brings joy to the heart and the world. It is unapologetic and life-changing. When two people share and experience authentic love, they become a light of hope for the world. Their love is a testament to the dignity of the human person and to the fact that a person's worth is not in how they look or what they can do but in who they are.

But I had not yet learned all of this, and once I had a boyfriend, my life was consumed by him. Everywhere he went, I went. I listened to his music, hung out with his friends, and started paying attention to his sports. I lost myself in my relationship with him. The people and things that were once important to me played second fiddle to my boyfriend. I pretty much checked out mentally from most of my school and home responsibilities. Everything I did was influenced by my relationship.

The attention he gave me just made me crave more of it. His affections were never enough to satisfy the deep longings in my heart I wanted him to fill. Even when he told me he loved me, I still doubted him or was worried that he soon would not love me anymore. Our relationship felt like a temporary love, one I had to continue buying on a daily basis with my attentiveness to my outward appearance and his desires. It seemed that each day was a new day to prove my love or it would be lost.

My life at fifteen years old was hijacked by a relationship that was not rooted in truth or beauty, let alone faith or God. Instead, it was rooted in my emotions. And don't get me wrong—this guy was a good guy. It's not like he was sprouting horns and breathing fire. He was kind, close to his family, and tried his best to make me feel special. But I allowed my life to be consumed by the relationship. Everything was about him. *Everything.*

It was October when everything shifted. October is one of the best months in the American Midwest. The air is crisp, and the rolling hills of Missouri are covered with red, orange, and light green puffs of trees that invite you to cuddle up with a mug of hot apple cider and a soft blanket. The fall also marks the beginning of high school football and the annual homecoming dance.

Everything about the homecoming dance was important— who you went with, what you wore, and what party you got invited to afterward. I was lucky. I had a boyfriend, so most of my problems were solved, right? I had a date, someone to dance with, and parties to go to. My dress was beautiful, my hands were elegant with a pretty French manicure, and my shoes, of course, were amazing. Everything was falling into place for a magical evening.

But then, a few days before the homecoming dance weekend, my boyfriend's best friend walked out of class with me and asked me this question: "Are you ready for it?"

I quickly told him yes, assuming he meant the practical aspects of the dance—dress, shoes, and hair.

He had a puzzled look on his face and again said, "No, Leah, I mean *it*. Are you ready for *it*?"

That's when I realized I had no idea what he was talking about. It's not like I didn't know what sex was; I just never really thought about it, so it didn't register with me when he referenced it so vaguely. However, I didn't want to act like I didn't know what was going on. I was one of those kids who, if I didn't know something, just pretended to know until I figured out what that something really was. So I lied, big-time. "Oh yeah, I'm totally ready," I said, which only made the situation even weirder.

He backed away slowly—didn't even respond—and, to be honest, I was happy about that. I didn't know and didn't care what he was talking about, so I went on with my day . . . until after lunch when my basketball team captain came up to me and said she had heard that I didn't know what "it" was. I laughed and told her of course I knew what it was. She called my bluff and said, "Then tell me, Leah, right now." As I stammered with embarrassment, she interrupted me. "Leah, 'it' is sex! I can't believe you didn't know that!" I was embarrassed. I tried to laugh it off, but inside I was scared, alarmed, and nervous.

I was raised in a Catholic Christian home. My parents are

really good people—faithful, prayerful, patient, funny, and mostly normal. They never gave me and my five brothers and sisters any rules that were beyond the norm or unrealistic. Their rules made practical sense—eat your vegetables, don't ride your bike through cow manure, and don't let your little brother eat his boogers—all of which were good but weren't exactly rules with life-changing consequences if they weren't followed. So I didn't really question when they spoke of sex as being only for a husband and a wife, but I also didn't understand what role God and faith had in it or how serious the implications were should I choose not to follow their guidance.

My boyfriend never mentioned sex to me himself. He used his friends to find out what my thoughts were on it. His best friend told me, "I think it's time to put the nail in the coffin." Funny how he said it was time, as if it were already past due when we had only been dating for three months. Also funny how he related sex to death—"put the nail in the coffin." But it seemed to me then that sex was a litmus test. If I really loved my boyfriend, if I was really committed, then I would offer my physical body. I would have sex.

Sex was the commerce used to validate both me and the relationship itself, but what I didn't quite realize was how giving in to this would only prove that our relationship and our desires were really just about physical beauty and not about love. How mismatched it was to think that love, which is something eternal and immaterial, must be proved and legitimized by something temporary and physical.

But the main thought running through my head was that

saying no meant putting my relationship in jeopardy. It was a choice I had to make. At the same time, just thinking about sex was uncomfortable. So I decided to put off thinking more deeply about it and instead to make a game-time decision when or if the opportunity presented itself. This was easier than contemplating the immensity of what it would mean to have sex with my boyfriend, lose my virginity, ignore my parents and my upbringing, and, ultimately, sever my relationship with God.

Homecoming night came faster than I expected, and before I knew it, I was home getting ready and waiting anxiously for my boyfriend to ring the doorbell. When he arrived, he placed the flower corsage on my wrist. I felt beautiful. And, as a couple, we looked beautiful together.

We took the obligatory picture in front of the fireplace to make my parents happy. My mom and dad were smiling, looking proud, and told me to have fun but to be careful. I promised them I would, but I lied. I knew what they meant by "be careful." They meant not to get into trouble, not to do something I would regret or that would go against the faith and morals they had taught me. I knew what they meant. But I also knew what my boyfriend expected of me.

The homecoming dance itself was fun. I danced with my boyfriend and with my girlfriends, and it was exactly what high school dances should be. After it ended my boyfriend and I attended an after-party, which my parents knew about, and then we snuck out of that party and went to another where there was no parental supervision.

It was there that I had to make my game-time decision: Would I have sex with my boyfriend or not? Unfortunately, because I had never talked about it with him or spent time thinking about what I truly wanted, he had gone ahead and set up a space and atmosphere where sex was anticipated and encouraged.

I hate disappointing people. I love making people happy, making them laugh or feel better about themselves or life altogether. And while some may call it a weakness, I had always seen it as a strength. And it was . . . until I began ignoring myself for the sake of others, placing myself in danger to fulfill someone else's momentary happiness. That's when it became not just a weakness but a grave threat to my health, identity, and emotional well-being.

In that moment it felt like the only choice was to love my boyfriend, and sex meant I loved him. If I chose not to have sex, that would mean I would have to explain myself and convince him that I did love him but just didn't want to have sex. That didn't make much sense to me, in light of the way I connected what I had to give physically with value, sex with love. I was running out of time to decide what to do. I was so nervous; I felt rushed. And then it happened; I gave myself away.

I lost my virginity at fifteen years old. I gave away something to someone who never deserved it, did not earn it, and would not keep it.

Immediately after, I went to the bathroom. There, I locked the door behind me and turned on the faucet so he wouldn't hear me cry. I slid down the bathroom door slowly.

I couldn't stop the tears. I felt an incredible weight of regret and hopelessness. I knew right away I should not have had sex with him; my desire to be loved had driven me into a situation where love was the last thing I found. Fear became my companion. I was scared. Scared of what to do next. Scared of the possibility of being pregnant or of contracting a sexually transmitted disease. Scared of my parents finding out. Scared of God forsaking me. I was even scared of showing my fear to my boyfriend in case he mistook it for me not loving him and thus regretting having sex. But the truth was I did regret it. There was something terribly wrong with how I thought of love and worth. I'd gotten it all backward.

I had been looking to my boyfriend and to the relationship itself to give me the love, acceptance, and sense of personal value I craved. And so I was willing to use my physical beauty to stabilize our relationship when it suddenly felt endangered. But this was the opposite of how God designed it to be. Our relationships with others can't be the source of our identity and worth; they will never be able to shoulder that weight for us. Instead, we must find worth and acceptance in God alone, whose love is not predicated on what we can offer him or how attractive we are. When we have this foundation, our relationships then have the freedom to blossom into expressions of the love and sacrifice that Jesus has already given us, seen beautifully in the sacrament of marriage, the benchmark of love that we should hold our partners to before we ask for physical unity.

Predictably, it wasn't more than two weeks after my fateful decision that my boyfriend and I broke up. The stress from sex, fear of pregnancy, lies I had told my parents, my newly depressed mood, the distance now between me and God because I feared I wasn't worthy of forgiveness—all of it had taken a toll. The desires in my heart to be wanted, to be seen as beautiful, to be loved—all those things that had factored into my decision to give my body to my boyfriend—were crushed. Our relationship wasn't prepared to handle life after sex because sex was not the answer to my questions of "Am I loved? Am I beautiful?" So we broke up. And I was left wondering if I ever really loved him and if he ever really loved me.

We both clearly did not understand what love really is.

So what is it? One of the best definitions of love I have read since my conversion comes from the philosopher and theologian Thomas Aquinas, who defined love as desiring the greatest good for the beloved.[1] The book of Exodus says similarly that love is wanting what is best for the one you love: "Thou hast led in thy steadfast love the people whom thou hast redeemed, thou hast guided them by thy strength to thy holy abode" (15:13). God, because of his love for his people, led them to their final home because it was best for them—their greatest good—to live in the land that God had prepared for them. The promised land in the Old Testament is an analogy for heaven; to be led to the promised land is to be led to God.

Love isn't merely a feeling; it is a desire to seek the good of the one you love. To say "I love you" means "I'm going to do everything in my power to do what is best for you." When we love someone, we want their greatest good, and as Christians we know that our greatest good is God alone. "Jesus replied: 'Love the Lord your God with all your heart and with all your soul and with all your mind'" (Matt. 22:37 NIV). If God is the greatest good, love in its most final and perfect form is wanting yourself and others to be as close to God as possible.

How would you define love? I encourage you to take some time to explore your definition of that term; see if it matches up more with what the world says or with what God says. Consider this carefully, especially if your definition is closer to the world's. Christ told us in John 15:19, "Because you are not of the world, but I chose you out of the world, therefore the world hates you." The world does not love us, so why take its advice on love?

After the homecoming dance, people began to talk in my high school. Soon the whole school found out that I'd had sex with my boyfriend and that not long after that we'd broken up. We weren't the beautiful couple that others envied anymore. I was hurt and angry, and I tried to cover it up by acting like I didn't care or wasn't bothered by losing my virginity to someone who was no longer in my life, someone who had used my body but had not really loved me in the end. He had not acted for my good. My conception of who I was and how much I was worth loving took a hit, but I pretended I was fine. This became my new normal. From that point onward, I hid my true self, my fear, and my hurt. In the end, giving all of me resulted in losing myself.

The opposite of love is not hate; it is use. Use is the abuse of love; in fact, it betrays love. When we use another person, we place their needs below our own, but worse yet, we place their value and dignity below ours. Often when we talk about being "used" we are referring to men using women, but women can be just as guilty of this. While men might use women for physical or sexual gain, women tend to use men for emotional gain, to increase their self-esteem. If I'm honest with myself, this was exactly how I had been using my boyfriend. He used me for his physical pleasure, and I used him to boost my feeling of worth. Interestingly, a study showed that girls with high self-esteem are three times more likely to delay sexual intercourse than girls with low self-esteem.[2] To me, this demonstrates that women who know their own worth realize that sex is not the answer to gaining it.

Another less commonly considered manifestation of use comes in the form of us chasing personal beauty as the world defines it. It is a kind of idol worship. We worship ourselves and our own physical beauty. And if we're not beautiful, we do everything we can to become so. Just as the ancient pagans offered prayers and sacrifices to gods who didn't exist, we offer time and money to the idol of our own beauty to feel a heightened sense of value. We use ourselves for the sake of ourselves. How twisted is that? We don't even love ourselves well, let alone others, and all so we can chase after a fleeting and false concept of worth and love.

The antidote to this worldview is knowing and believing that God created us out of his infinite love and that there is nothing we can do to merit his affection; there is no way we can become more attractive or increase our significance in his eyes. Not only did we do nothing to deserve his love, but we did a whole lot to reject it—yet Christ loves us. With this confidence in his unchangeable love, we can stop striving for what we already have and start living the life we were made for: a life worthy of the dignity with which we were created. Unfortunately, this was not the path I took.

What resulted from my decision the night of homecoming was this: I redefined love to fit my decisions and my new lifestyle and to cover up my regret. Rather than living out the truth that love is a choice to act for another's good, I chose to live as if love was just a feeling. If I didn't feel "in love," there was no love. My new definition made love just an effect of biochemistry. If the right hormones were in place, I was in love. If not, then I wasn't. So things like lack of sleep, not eating well, being stressed—all of which are known to throw off our biochemistry—impacted how I felt toward people. It is a sad definition of love when the loss of a little sleep can have such an impact.

Because this definition of love I adopted was purely physical, love was anything that made me feel good, and I loved whoever or whatever made me feel good. If love was merely an emotion, a mix of physiological processes in the body, then it made sense that it needed to be validated by other physical acts—particularly the act of sex, in which, in the right circumstances, we get an emotional and biological high. But seeking these emotional and biological highs wasn't seeking love; it was seeking my own pleasure, which was a form of self-worship. By limiting love to a mere physical act,

I detached love from its highest calling, which is to desire the good for *others*.

In doing this, I lied to myself. And this lie about love bled into my conceptions of sex and beauty too. Love became consumeristic for me. I shopped for love; I was both the customer and the product. I told myself that sex was no big deal, just a part of everyday relationships, and that using my body would help me attract love. This consumerist mind-set transformed beauty into a tool that would help me find what I wanted so badly. And so I pursued beauty in my pursuit of love.

The desire for beauty is not a bad thing. It is built into us by God to lead us toward love, because love *is* beautiful. We know intuitively that beauty should lead to love. Theologian and philosopher Augustine of Hippo recognized this in the fourth century: "It is not possible to love what is not beautiful."[3] We don't love ugly things. Even if we are mistaken about something's beauty, we need to believe it is beautiful if we are to love it. But sometimes we are seduced into thinking something is beautiful that really isn't. And often this happens because we have a faulty definition of love.

Imagine being cold and lost in a forest. From a distance you see smoke. You know the smoke is a sign that there is fire and warmth somewhere close, so you follow it. Beauty is also like a smoke signal; we follow it to find love. However, imagine following the smoke only to find that it is coming from a broken-down tractor that isn't giving off much heat. Perhaps you should have known that machine smoke was blacker than wood smoke, but you didn't. Similarly, we need to be wary of the different kinds of beauty in the world and what kinds of love they indicate—where their smoke signals lead.

If my definition of love is physical, I will be attracted primarily to physical beauty. However, if my definition of love is God's definition—that love is desiring good for others—then I will be attracted to people who love in this way, even if they are physically ugly.

The beauty I was attracted to—or the smoke I was following—was a kind that revealed a bad understanding of love. When looking for love, I looked only at the exterior beauty of a man and was not too concerned about his heart or future plans. On the other side of things, I personally gave off false smoke signals. I thought that if I looked beautiful, men would notice, and then I could find love. My beauty was like a billboard: "Available for love! I come with emotional and physical benefits." But the sort of men I attracted with that message were not able to love me as I should have been loved.

Love and beauty are so closely tied to each other that they can't help but affect each other. When love becomes warped, so does beauty. If we choose to define love by a mere physical act, it's logical that our ideas about beauty will follow, as we'll view it as a crucial tool in our ongoing efforts to secure worth and validation. When love is not focused on the good of another person as it ought to be, but rather on our own emotional highs, beauty, too, becomes inwardly focused. It is a lonely existence.

To avoid feeling alone when I was in the middle of my

misunderstanding about love and beauty, I began to align myself with the world. I surrounded myself with people who thought the same way I did about sex, love, and beauty. Ironically, even while being surrounded by like-minded people, I never felt lonelier. I bought and read all the magazines that supported my ideology. *Cosmopolitan* became my go-to for beauty and relationship advice, and, together with my friends, I entered into the Me religion, where I placed myself at the center of the universe. I made every decision in reference to me alone rather than to others or God. My god was Me.

But this was mainly a front I put up. At the core of this transition was a great fear that my worth had diminished. If my boyfriend, to whom I had given everything, didn't love me, how could my family love me? How could God love me? I was afraid my parents would reject me if they found out what I had done. I was afraid God would not forgive me. I did not think I belonged to my family or my church community anymore. My parents were the ones who had sat in the same pew every Sunday, led Bible studies, and earnestly loved the Lord. How could I disappoint them? As for God, I believed he would forgive everyone else but me. I was certain that I would lose all my value in my parents' eyes, as well as God's, if they knew what I had done. I wouldn't be beautiful to them anymore.

I should have known better. I came from a good, intact, faithful family, and yet I didn't think God would truly show me mercy or make me new again after I had messed up. In reality, I was doubting God's power—Christ's death, resurrection, and the new life he promises to all who believe in him and love him—because I'd bought into another way of thinking.

As a little girl I was scared of monsters. My parents told me they didn't exist. How I wish they would have told me the whole truth. Monsters do exist; they're just not hiding in closets. They're standing in the light of day. They are found within us in lies, doubt, fear, and unreachable expectations of beauty that we think will earn us love. Make no mistake, monsters are real. And we must fight them. We must go to battle and bravely face what seeks to destroy us.

This is a fight we face every day—on multiple fronts. Western culture elevates the physical as the bar for pleasure, beauty, and love. The damage this causes affects nearly everyone one way or another. Everything from our physical beauty to our relationships, jobs, faith, and even our dreams are affected by this ideology. It all must look good—and by this I mean it all must look trendy and worthy of a social media post. On average, 93 million selfies are taken around the world each day.[4] Talk about a fixation on how we look! But it is no wonder when we have been told over and over that our appearance is our key to acceptance.

Every person wants to be valued and loved. Love is the most basic longing of the human heart. Your definition of love will shape your whole life. It will be the foundation of your understanding of God and your own self-worth; it will choose your spouse and your friends. It will be the reason you stand up for the underdog or become the bully. Let me ask you again:

What is your definition of love? In high school, it seemed to me that love was all about how others made me feel, and in my mind, there was a clear connection between how much affection I got from others and how I looked—so I equated the two. Beauty was my key to love. It would take a lightning-bolt moment and a whole new perspective on love and beauty, identity and worth, before I finally came to see the truth and started discovering what God had to say about all this.

Understanding the correct definition of love is not a cure-all, but it does give us a concrete, real, and truthful place to start. Once we know it, we can go back and examine if a person or relationship is in alignment with God's definition of love for us. Without it, we flounder and can end up accepting the opposite of love (use) as the real thing.

Maybe you have never encountered imitation love, or maybe you found yourself somewhere in my story. No matter. Accepting and surrendering our lives to the God of love is transformative for all of us. When we do, we discover that love has a name, a face, and that is Christ Jesus. Jesus tells us, "This is my commandment, that you love one another as I have loved you" (John 15:12 ESV). In the end, nothing else will matter and nothing else will remain except love in its truest form. Loving ourselves and others as God commands opens us up to a life rooted in truth and makes a way to authentic beauty.

4

THE TRUTH ABOUT BEAUTY

TRUE, AUTHENTIC BEAUTY ISN'T PRIMARILY what we see with our eyes. Mother Teresa of Calcutta was not a particularly physically beautiful person to look at. Her hands were worn, and her feet were actually rather disfigured from the poor shoes she always wore. As she aged, she became permanently hunched over due to all the time she spent bending and serving the poor. Yet all who met her have described her as beautiful.

Author, speaker, and television host Susan Conroy met Mother Teresa, and the encounter changed her life. Susan said,

> I had never met anyone in my life as humble as Mother Teresa. She was as humble as the poor whom we would lift up out of the gutters. Her humility was strikingly beautiful to me. Mother Teresa embodied so many other qualities as well, qualities that are all too rare in the world

today. I wished that I could have brought her home with me, shown her to everyone, and said: "Just look at her!" Her appearance, her spirit, and her presence spoke a thousand words about integrity, about God, about true beauty, about inner strength, about love.[1]

What was the beauty people saw in this small, wrinkled woman? I believe the beauty they saw was the love of Christ made manifest in the flesh of Mother Teresa. She was beautiful because she loved. She loved because Christ loved her, as he does all of us. Mother Teresa lived her life with a deep awareness of God's love for her and God's presence in everyone she met. She often said that the poor were Jesus in disguise. She firmly believed she was caring for Jesus himself in every single man, woman, and child she encountered. This made her beautiful. Not her figure, not her clothes, but her heart on fire with the light of Christ. Unfortunately, more often than not, we struggle to live with this kind of true beauty.

Human beings are physical creatures. We have bodies and senses. We can't help but notice other people: if they are tall or short, if they are wearing expensive clothes or not, or if their hair is blown out or a mess. This is all very human. It is hard not to get distracted by it all and not to judge others based on their external appearance because that is what we notice first.

But if we focus our attention only on the external, we will miss the beauty of people like Mother Teresa. We will miss the bigger picture and the point of beauty in the first place.

So, as we seek to understand the essence of beauty as God created it and designed it to be—rather than look for direction from the guidance of current fashion professionals, who are more than slightly biased toward the external—let's instead consider the thoughts of some respected philosophers who have been mulling over the definition of beauty for thousands of years. We'll also take a look at Scripture, which will help us understand what God has to say on the subject.

Philosophers

What exactly is beauty? It is difficult to give a definition because beauty is such a fundamental concept. Often when we're asked what beauty is, we just point to something that is beautiful and say *that* is beauty. Thomas Aquinas, a twelfth-century Dominican priest, carefully pondered this question of how to define or describe beauty. While he didn't give an essential definition, he did say that beauty is "that which pleases upon being seen."[2] On first read, it might seem like he is just as exterior focused as the beauty industry. However, as we dig a little deeper, we will see he had something very different in mind.

The kind of "being seen" that Aquinas talked about is not the same as having good eyesight. Rather, it refers to knowledge, to comprehension. In other words beauty is "that which pleases upon being known." It pleases not just upon being physically seen, but rather upon being deeply seen with the heart. Being known goes beyond the physical and encompasses the beauty of speech, actions, and existence.

The other word Aquinas used in his definition of beauty is *pleases*, and that means more than just a sensual pleasure like taste or touch. It is better translated from the Latin as "a delight for the soul." So we could say that beauty is "that which delights the soul upon being known." And this explains the beauty of Mother Teresa; she didn't delight our sense of sight upon being seen, but rather she delighted our souls upon being known.

This definition of beauty is very important because it helps us understand that beauty is primarily a reality that stirs our souls, our inmost beings, not just our senses.

In addition to this definition of beauty, Aquinas, following the tradition of Greek philosophers, identified three qualities that are found in everything that is beautiful: integrity, proportion, and clarity.[3] These three qualities will be present, he argued, in beautiful objects, actions, and beings. It is important to have some consistent markers of beauty so that we have standards for beauty; otherwise, how will we know the difference between imitation and authentic beauty? Remember, these qualities apply not just to physical appearance but to beauty of speech, action, and existence.

Integrity, as Aquinas thought about it, was in reference to wholeness as opposed to dividedness or brokenness. I'm sure this is one of the reasons why women don't like seeing other women portrayed as objects in advertising, as we discussed in chapter 1. When this happens there is a focus on only one aspect of the women being portrayed, and they lose their depth and nuance. There is a lack of integrity, or the unity of all that makes them who they are, in this kind of presentation. We inherently want to be whole, to be exactly as God created us to be from the beginning, with all our complexities; therefore, we like to see things whole and unified and find beauty in this kind of completeness.

Think about integrity in your own life. What attracts you? Do you see a unity and wholeness present in these people and things? That desire for integrity has been present in us since the garden of Eden; it's a yearning for things to be perfect, as God meant them to be.

The second aspect of beauty is proportion. Proportion is the relation between parts of a whole. Ancient Greek sculptors were obsessed with proportion. The sculpted head had to be in proper proportion relative to the torso, the arms to the legs, and so on. This proportion is called *the golden ratio*. Researchers at Stanford have defended this idea of proportion as a desirable physical characteristic by performing studies on the human response to symmetry.[4] Symmetry is extremely attractive and pleasing to the human eye. Babies spend more time staring at pictures of symmetrical faces than asymmetrical ones, and men consistently rank women as most beautiful who are the most symmetrical.[5]

But beyond physical proportion, there is a beauty in immaterial proportions as well. Ancient Greek philosophers looked for proportion in the actions of a person's life. If you are generous one day but cowardly the next, there is no proportion among your virtues. A beautiful person should be symmetrically good, that is, good in all ways.

The third aspect of beauty, clarity, is a kind of radiance or splendor that beauty has. It is a manifestation of the essence of someone or something. It is what radiates from a woman— her "womanness"—or an apple its "appleness." Think about a time when you saw a beautiful thing and your breath was taken away. That was your reaction to the clarity of that beautiful thing, the splendor it had simply in its being.

One example of when I experienced the clarity of beauty is the time I stood at the south rim of the Grand Canyon. It was early in the morning and still dark. Ricky, my soon-to-be-husband, and I were there together, waiting for the sun to rise. The canyon was cold and quiet. Snow was atop the trees, and the river down below looked gray. As the sun began to rise, the rays hit the canyon, and in minutes it lit up with every color of the rainbow. The once cold and dark canyon literally shone with layers of red, orange, purple, and yellow. The river was a greenish blue, and the sky could not have been bluer. It was the most beautiful sight my eyes had ever seen, and I held my breath as the rising sun gradually uncovered it bit by bit. I was stunned, speechless, and in awe. It was wholly and purely what God had made it to be, and that radiated a natural beauty that could not be enhanced by anything beyond its simple existence.

While integrity, proportion, and clarity can be applied to physical objects, their application to existence and spiritual concepts is far more important. After all, we are living in a fallen world, so the outer shell that we see does not always match the inner reality. Archbishop Fulton Sheen incisively said, "The beauty on the outside never gets into the soul. But the beauty of the soul reflects itself on the face."[6] Sheen recognized that there isn't a necessary relationship between our external beauty and our internal beauty. As great as our physical beauty might be, it can't impact the internal beauty of our soul.

On the other hand, the internal beauty of our soul actually can impact our external beauty. For example, some of my daughter's paintings end up as swirly dark messes that resemble black holes in the universe. In themselves, they don't exactly exude wholeness, a sense of right proportion, or a particular radiance, and they will never find their way into the Louvre. However, I find them beautiful because she made them as a gift for me. They have a quality that goes beyond the surface, and when I see their swirly, messy shapes, I see works of beauty that delight my soul.

When was the last time something delighted your soul? I hope recently! Because your soul is that part of you that will live forever. It is that part of you that God himself created and infused in your body. All our actions, our whole lives, should be most concerned with the condition and beauty of our souls. What does it mean for our souls to be beautiful and to inspire delight in the souls of others? For an answer to this question, let us turn to Scripture.

Scripture

You might be surprised to find out that God has said quite a lot about beauty. To begin, let's first look at how beauty is ascribed to God. The psalmist in Psalm 27 says his ultimate desire is to see the Lord's beauty.

> One thing have I asked of the LORD,
>> that will I seek after;
> that I may dwell in the house of the LORD
>> all the days of my life,
> to behold the beauty of the LORD,
>> and to inquire in his temple. (v. 4)

What does it mean to behold the beauty of the Lord? Thomas Dubay, a theologian of the twentieth century, pointed out in his book *The Evidential Power of Beauty* that in Scripture beauty is a synonym for God's glory.[7] So what we mean when we say "That is beautiful!" is actually "That reflects the glory of God!"

The one person in all of human history who perfectly revealed God's glory and made beauty concrete in all its fullness was Jesus. The beauty he displayed was that unearthly kind of beauty, the kind that doesn't necessarily present itself on a physical level. Throughout the Bible we see several references juxtaposing outward appearance to the condition of the heart. In Matthew 23:27, for example, Jesus rebuked the religious elite, saying, "Woe to you, scribes and Pharisees, hypocrites! for you are like whitewashed tombs, which outwardly appear beautiful, but within they are full of dead men's bones and all uncleanness." Jesus is clear: one can indeed be outwardly beautiful, only to be filled with no inner beauty, but rather ugliness.

Or again, in 1 Samuel, we see God speaking to the prophet Samuel, instructing him how to recognize the king that God has anointed, and it has nothing to do with how he looks: "Do not consider his appearance or his height, for I have rejected him. The LORD does not look at the things people look at. People look at the outward appearance, but the LORD looks at the heart" (16:7 NIV).

Even the Old Testament prophecies about the coming Messiah stressed that we could not rely on outward appearance to recognize Jesus: "He had no form or comeliness that we should look at him, / and no beauty that we should desire him" (Isa. 53:2). Not even the long-awaited Messiah, God made man, would be recognized by his physical beauty.

Jesus, in his person and in his life, exuded the other side of beauty, that is, the inner beauty of the soul. His beauty and God's glory were revealed in how much he loved. His time here on earth was filled with caring for his people out of a loving heart, pointing people to the truth that would save them. Or, in other words, desiring and acting for their greatest good. Pope Benedict XVI affirmed the special relationship between truth, love, and beauty when he described beauty as "the splendour of the truth and the flowering of Love."[8] Not surprisingly then, Jesus' beauty is essentially related to love.

He was beautiful because he loved his people to the end. "But God demonstrates his own love for us in this: While we were still sinners, Christ died for us" (Rom. 5:8 NIV). As the Savior who redeemed the world, he *is* love.

We are created in the image and likeness of a God who is love, who loves us, and who wants us to share in his love. It is by sharing in God's love that we give glory to him and reflect his beauty in the world. The truth is all about love. And beauty is what draws us to see both truth and love in reality and in God.

Despite our failings, Jesus showed his love for us through the most beautiful moment in human history—his death on a cross. While it seems counterintuitive initially to call a moment that involved such intense suffering beautiful, when we actually think about that act, it makes sense. That moment was the manifestation of the radical truth of the Father's great love for all human beings, as he sent his only Son to die for us in the ultimate act of love for you and me. If that moment on the cross was the most truthful and loving moment in all of history, then, by definition, it was also the most beautiful.

The world's focus on external beauty often keeps us from making the connection between beauty and God. But we've been made with a body *and* a soul, where the Holy Spirit lives and dwells within us. As the apostle Paul noted in 1 Corinthians 6:19, "Do you not know that your body is a temple of the Holy Spirit within you, which you have from God?" Authentic beauty must take into account what is within us even more so than what is on the outside. It is a reflection of God, the source of love, truth, and beauty. So beauty in all its forms should remind us of God, not ourselves.

What we see in Hollywood and in the majority of fashion images is the idol of imitation beauty, a beauty loved for itself and not for its creator. It is like cotton candy: big, fluffy, and sweet, making your mouth water when you see it but revealing itself to be empty and short of satisfying once you dive deeper into it. Those images are literally false, from the "frankensteining" and retouching of Photoshop to the false eyelashes that make the models' eyes pop. There is nothing true about them and therefore nothing inherently beautiful. Imitation beauty fizzles and fades, but true beauty remains because it is rooted in God himself.

Authentic beauty at its core is a reflection of God's love in the world, and it naturally draws those who come into contact with it to God. In this way beauty is essentially evangelical. It draws each of us in, and insofar as we live beautiful lives, we participate in God's mission to draw others to him. We find this message all over the Bible.

Ephesians 2:10 tells us that each one of us is God's artwork that ought to lead to good: "For we are his workmanship, created in Christ Jesus for good works, which God prepared beforehand, that we should walk in them." Clearly, Paul is saying that we were made by God to manifest his goodness in the world.

Romans 10:15 says, "As it is written, 'How beautiful are the feet of those who preach good news,'" and Psalm 50:2 says, "Out of Zion, the perfection of beauty, God shines forth." The feet of those who preach the good news are necessarily beautiful as they reflect the glory and the good news of God in the world, which is the very definition of beauty! And Zion, the city on a hill, which is God's resting place, also manifests the beauty of God.

And again in 2 Corinthians, "And we all who, with our unveiled faces like mirrors reflecting the glory of the Lord, are being transformed into the image that we reflect in brighter and brighter glory; this is the working of the Lord who is Spirit" (3:18). Paul was saying that God's glory is manifested in the world primarily through us, through the transformation of our hearts. In other words, as Irenaeus said, "The glory of God is man fully alive."[9] This is an incredible mission that each of us is called to take up: to manifest in our own lives God's glory and to be reflectors of his beauty in the world.

As beauty is an attribute of God, that natural desire we all have to reach out for it is actually a desire for him. We want our love, our work, and ultimately our lives to be beautiful. This type of beauty goes beyond a fashion trend and points to the eternal. God invites us to live out his definition of beauty, so dramatically on display in the face of his Son on the cross of Calvary, beauty that transcends the world as we know it. It's an invitation to embrace lives that point beyond ourselves to God, beautiful lives that delight the soul and reflect his glory. The question is, will we accept his invitation?

～ 5 ～

DESIRING BEAUTY

Why We Don't and How We Can

THE FIRST TIME I REALIZED I WASN'T LIVING A life of authentic beauty, it wasn't because of anything I did. Although I was unhappy and dissatisfied with my life at the time, I wasn't actively looking for answers or for an alternate way of living. It's not like I sat down to read a philosophy book on beauty that changed me. Instead, beauty came looking for me.

I can still smell the cigarette smoke through the rose-scented lotion on the makeup artist's hands and hear the loud thud of the large AC unit turning on. I can feel that fireball of anxiety in the pit of my stomach and the cold sweat beginning as I fumbled through the clothes that were brought in for the photo shoot. I was nervous because I felt overwhelmingly uncomfortable for some reason that day. Nervous because I was afraid they would find out I was not as beautiful as I was pretending to be. I was trying to act like I'd done this a million times before, ironically acting empowered by choosing to be objectified. But deep down I wanted to run. I wanted to quit but thought to myself, *Leah, this is what most people would die for. You don't say no to this kind of stuff.* And so I continued on in fear, trying to make others value me.

I finally picked out an outfit—and by outfit I mean a coordinated set of lingerie, all of it see-through, all of it humiliating. But the worst part was still to come. After I was dressed, if you can call it dressed, I had to walk across the large warehouse floor to the set, about three hundred feet away. Every eye was on me, the eyes of photographers, assistants, stylists, and random others, while I nervously walked in high heels, lingerie, and a half smile to the area marked for the shoot. Every single one of my insecurities was screaming inside my head, those I had brought with me to New York and the ones that were created after being on *America's Next Top Model.*

No one tells you about the aftermath of being on a national reality TV show. The comments online were beyond negative. They were downright dehumanizing. People on completely different continents from me had an opinion on my beauty and my value. I wasn't just being judged by the judges' panel; the world judged me. I read every single one of the comments, hoping that maybe just one person would have something kind to say. But for the few "I think she's pretty" comments, dozens more said, "She's boring, too normal, ugly, why would they even pick her?" Other comments went beyond the bounds of judging my beauty and attacked me personally, saying I was a "whore," "not worthy of living," "she should kill herself," and "a waste of earth space." I wish I could forget them. I wish I had never read them. Instead, they stayed with me as new insecurities, bonding with my old ones and swirling endlessly through my mind.

I probably looked scared, naive, and desperate as I tried to figure out how to get into a pose that was sexy and sultry for the shoot. I was trying to look like I had "more to offer," like they had told me on the phone when they gave me the job. But instead, I was desperately attempting to look like and be something I was not made to be.

We are not made to be objectified. We are not made to be used. We are not made to be entertainment. We are made to love and be loved. We are made for God. The realization of this truth was about to hit me in just a few short minutes. God was priming my heart for himself. He was allowing me to feel the effects of a life led without him: the loneliness, the ugliness, and the constant need for love and approval.

As the photo shoot began, I could feel the eyes of everyone on my body, and I hated it. I wanted out. I was beginning to see the truth of my life and did not like it. I hated the fact that I had willingly chosen this. Not just the photo shoot, but my entire lifestyle. No one had forced me to accept the standard of beauty that basically made me question every inch of body, made me jealous of others, and made me feel the insatiable need to always have more, to look better. No one had forced me to accept imitation love, give myself away, or live in a state of constant fear of unintended pregnancies, diseases, or the ending of a relationship. No one had forced me to chase the dream of being on the cover of a magazine just so I could validate my existence or banish my insecurities. I. Chose. This. I chose a life that was built on lies.

There was no reason why I had to give myself away to keep a relationship or prove my love. There was no reason why I should have lowered God's standard of beauty to match the world's materialistic form of it. There was no reason why I should have desired to be known to the world while neglecting to be known by the One who loved me first.

The photographer kept clicking picture after picture, and then it happened. My eyes inadvertently met the flash, and I needed a quick break to regain my focus. I paused and looked away, blinking. During those twenty seconds, I saw the most startling, unexpected thing. I saw a vision of myself wearing the outfit I was modeling, as if a little movie was playing. I noticed my hands were cupped and held together at my waist, and then I raised them upward to the level of my head. At that point I saw the shadowy profile of a man's face; he looked at my hands and then bowed his head sadly. In response a strong feeling of disappointment covered me like a blanket. I quickly brought my hands back down to see what was so disappointing. And that's when I saw it. The reason for so many of my problems was in my hands: *my hands were empty*.

Chasing external beauty all those years had left me with nothing. My worth, up until that moment, had been found in the world and its definition of beauty. But God does not value us because of our external beauty. Holding up my hands was like holding up my heart to God, and the truth in that moment was that my heart was ugly. I was self-centered, and my lifestyle was proof of the selfish life I had been leading. I had used people to help me move up the social and professional ladders so I could feel valued. I had used boyfriends to help me feel loved. I had used every good thing God gave me in an ugly way.

When I saw myself in that flash with empty hands raised to Jesus, I realized that although God had offered me the best gift in the universe, his very own love, I had lived as if he didn't exist. I had rejected his love. Those empty hands were a sad depiction of my life, very much like the prodigal son coming home to his father after spending all of his inheritance and having nothing to offer but himself. And here I thought the world would make me feel full, loved, and satisfied. Instead, like my hands, I felt empty.

In the same moment that I noticed my hands were empty, five simple words were spoken to my heart that changed everything: "I made you for more." Over and over I heard it, like an echo. "I made you for more. I made you for more. I made you for more." I wanted to deny it and think I was just making it up. That would have been the easy thing to do, to tell myself that it was just my nerves or the result of a bad ham sandwich, anything but the truth. But I couldn't. I knew the vision was true. And I knew its message was true as well: I *was* made for more.

I was not made to be used like an object. I was made to

love and to be loved. I was made to be beautiful, to be the manifestation of God's glory in the world.

All this happened in a matter of seconds, and I was startled when the photographer began snapping his fingers, trying to get me back into position to restart the shoot. But I couldn't. What had just happened to my heart could not be ignored. I told him I had to go and that I was done. He then told me that most girls feel like this and that over time, "You'll get used to it."

But I never wanted to get used to that feeling of being used. "No," I said, "I have to go." I quickly gathered my things, ignored everyone's pleas, and walked straight to the door.

Before I left, one of the photographers said, "If you leave, you'll be a nobody."

All I could say in reply was "Do you promise?"

When I walked out of the photo shoot, I'm sure the photographer and the others on set thought I was just some silly, simple girl who had gotten in too deep and wanted to run back home to Mommy and Daddy. And you know what? They were right. I was in too deep, in fact. I was drowning in the ridiculous notion that my worth solely lay in my exterior, and I was going to run home to God the Father so that he could put the broken pieces of my heart back together and so that he could remind me of who I was and what I was worth.

If it hadn't been for the miraculous grace of God, I might never have left the modeling world. I think back to my moment of conversion and wonder how I could have been so blind. Why couldn't I see earlier that my entire life was a disaster? Why had I settled for a relationship in which I gave all of me and got nothing in return? Why did I allow other people to dictate how I should look, what I should wear, or even what I should dream of?

And then I figured it out.

Fear

I had allowed four main things to keep me from living the life I was born to live, and fear was the first of them. Stupid, ugly, life-sucking fear had supported the many lies I believed: *You are only as good as how you look in the picture. To get his love, you'll have to give your body. If you gain weight, have an acne breakout, or if you don't wear the most fashion-forward clothes, your beauty and desirability will decline. Your value is based on what others think of you. You can't start over; just accept where you are in life. If you go home, you'll be a quitter.*

I was afraid of what people would say or think about me if they saw beneath my facade of braces-straightened teeth, carefully maintained weight, and Instagram-worthy life. I was afraid of being alone, of being found ugly and unworthy of love. I was afraid to stand up and demand true love and respect from others. I was afraid of failing. I was afraid God would not forgive me and would not love me. Afraid, afraid, afraid.

Everything in my life up to the moment of my realization I had done out of fear. Fear had been my daily motivator to stay on the path of self-destruction. I had refused to reflect, think, or meditate on anything spiritual or meaningful up until then because I knew deep down that once I was faced with truth, change would be inevitable. And I knew it would be painful to change since I had gone so far from the path God had set for me. The consequences were too great and too scary, so I refused to seek truth. I was not brave.

However, on that afternoon in New York City, in the middle of the photo shoot, truth smacked me right in the face. I could not deny it. Christ was speaking to my heart, reaching out to remind me of my worth and my dignity. I wanted the message I'd heard—"I made you for more"—to be true, but could it really be?

I knew that what I heard and saw during the photo shoot was real. It was not a lie. It was not fearmongering. It was truth wrapped in hope, a truth I had long forgotten. I had believed the world's idea of value would satisfy my desires, but it hadn't. This messy world could only offer the finite. God, and only God, can offer the infinite.

Those five simple words from Jesus changed my life. The truth I had been afraid of finding out—that beneath the surface I was unworthy and unlovable—wasn't the truth at all. The truth was that God loved me in spite of all I had done and failed to do. And even with my history, he still desired me and invited me to share his love. The words I heard that morning gave me hope and an almost immediate resurgence of courage. Truth—real truth—is exhilarating and liberating. I *was* made for more. It was time to act on it. It was time to be brave.

Walking out of that photo shoot and telling the photographer to go ahead and make me a nobody felt like something out of a movie. For the first time in ten years, I was honest with myself and courageously acted on the truth that Christ spoke to my heart. His grace was working within me, and it felt good and right. Hope spread through my heart like wildfire—hope that I could change *and* persevere in that change, that true beauty awaited me.

I can only imagine this is how the Samaritan woman must have felt after her encounter with Christ (see John 4:1–29). She, too, had not been living a life of beauty but one of sin and fear. People gossiped about her, and she probably had very few friends or none at all. I bet she felt as if she couldn't start over and in turn believed she was damaged goods, that the future was a hopeless unknown.

Until Christ.

Though she went to the well at noon to avoid people, when she saw Jesus there, she did not turn back in fear. Jesus offered her living water, that is, the grace, redemption, and salvation that removed the weight of all her mistakes. He reminded her that she was not made for a life of sin and regret but of *beauty*—sustaining, transformative beauty that draws people in and points back to the only true source of this living water.

What if she had given in to fear? What if she had turned around? At that well, the Samaritan woman had an encounter with beauty, with Jesus Christ. He was calling her to embrace him and his work of true beauty in her life. If she had given in to fear, if she hadn't been brave, she never would have discovered the freedom and joy he invites us all into.

Not only did this encounter with beauty affect the Samaritan woman, but it affected a whole village. After she spoke with Jesus and her heart was changed, she went back to her village to tell everyone about Jesus:

> Many Samaritans from that city believed in him because of the woman's testimony, "He told me all that I ever did." So when the Samaritans came to him, they asked him to stay with them; and he stayed there two days. And many more believed because of his word. (John 4:39–41)

If it had not been for that woman, a whole town would not have been converted! She had a great mission waiting for her once she overcame her fear and responded to the ache in her heart. Her mission was to be a mirror of the life-giving beauty and love of God and to invite others to join her in it.

All over the world women today feel the same suffering: The pain of being forgotten, lonely, isolated, and bullied. The echoes of regret, sin, and hurt. The sting of never feeling good enough. The nights lying awake wondering *if* God will forgive them and the fear of starting over.

Has fear kept you from being fully alive with Christ? Has doubt kept you from starting afresh? Has the world's standard of beauty or love kept you from seeing yourself as "wonderfully made" (Ps. 139:14 NIV) and called to something greater? Look back on your own life and see where Christ has called you to return to him and the life of hope and beauty he made you for. His plans and all he has in store for you are beyond what you can even guess.

Being willing to recognize the emptiness and suffering in our souls, though painful at first, is the first step in leading a truly beautiful life. So be brave, leave fear behind, and run toward beauty.

Noise

The second thing that tends to keep us from living the kind of life we were made for is, quite simply, noise. It is really hard to ignore all the voices of the world out there that are continually trying to sell us imitation beauty. Imitation beauty is everywhere: on the rack at the checkout counter in the grocery store, on billboards as we drive around town, on television and radio commercials, and even in the words and attitudes of people we know. How can we get away from it long enough to remind ourselves what it really means to be beautiful, what our identities are rooted in, and that we are worth so much more than what the world says we are?

The easiest way to combat noise, although probably the most uncomfortable one, is practicing silence. Silence and contemplation are lost arts in our busy world. We are connected to everyone and everything almost every second of the day. We don't dare leave our homes or offices without our cell phones. Even when we are surrounded by people we love and want to spend time with, we come down with an instant case of FOMO (fear of missing out) and consequently spend an unhealthy amount of time scrolling through our feeds, checking in with the world . . . just in case we might've missed something.

Don't get me wrong—I'm not saying we should all get rid of our pocket-sized tech gadgets. The rise of cell phones and social media has done a lot of good for the world. We can now easily communicate with family who live in other cities and stay connected better than ever before. By using social media I was able to call for the prayers of more than 150,000 people when my daughter was rushed to the hospital with a severe asthma attack. With the push of a button, Ricky and I have shared with our family thousands of miles away the good news of welcoming new babies into this world.

But cell phones and social media can also be a huge distraction when the world is just one swipe away. Our phones have become extensions of ourselves. The Pew Research Council found that among eighteen- to twenty-four-year-olds, 81 percent admit that they regularly check their phones for messages or missed calls, even when they haven't felt it vibrate or heard it ring.[1] We are so habituated to our phones' vibration or ringtone that we actually imagine it is there when it isn't. Sometimes we even treat our phones like lovers; 61 percent of the same age group admit that they sleep next to their phones so that they don't miss anything during the night.[2]

In the face of the twentieth century's distractions, German French artist Jean Arp observed,

Man has turned his back on silence. Day after day he invents machines and devices that increase noise and distract humanity from the essence of life, contemplation, meditation. . . . [T]ooting, howling, screeching, booming, crashing, whistling, grinding, and trilling bolster his ego.[3]

With so much noise, it is no wonder it is difficult to be silent. To be silent today means cutting off something that is almost a part of you—your phone—and retreating somewhere away from the noise. Today that takes intentional and near-heroic choices to do.

What's ironic is that in a world full of FOMO, we are definitely missing out on the most important things in life. The kingdom of God is quite contrary to the kingdom of noise. C. S. Lewis in his book *The Screwtape Letters* reveals how easy it is to get humans to forget their true identities, their worth, and even God. In it, Screwtape—a senior devil who is mentoring his nephew devil, Wormwood—offers guidance on how best to make sure we humans are too preoccupied to find our way to the silence and worship that reveal truth and call us higher:

Music and silence—how I detest them both! How thankful we should be that ever since our Father entered Hell—though longer ago than humans, reckoning in light years, could express—no square inch of infernal space and no moment of infernal time has been surrendered to either of those abominable forces, but all has been occupied by Noise—Noise, the grand dynamism, the audible expression of all that is exultant, ruthless, and virile—Noise which alone defends us from silly qualms, despairing scruples, and impossible desires. We will make the whole universe a noise in the end.[4]

Although published in 1942, long before the use of cell phones and social media, *The Screwtape Letters* shows that we as human beings always have and always will struggle with noise, wherever it comes from. We are always tempted to avoid silence, and this is a tragedy. Silence is the practice that can help us shut out all the mixed messages we receive from the world, and when we're left alone with ourselves, we can more clearly perceive both God's truth and our inner thoughts and feelings.

If we are brave enough, we should pray, "Lord, help me to see the truth about myself." This is a bold prayer because you might not like what you see. The truth can reveal ugliness, and it can be hard to change. But remember, beauty is the splendor of the truth. If we ask the Lord to reveal the truth about ourselves, what we are really asking is, "Lord, make me beautiful."

You might think I am counseling exactly what the beauty industry counsels—*look at your flaws; I have a solution that will change you!*—but reflecting on our spiritual flaws is not the same as the beauty industry exposing our physical flaws. The beauty industry exposes in order to enslave, to keep us always going back for more of the same "cures" because our "flaws" can never be completely fixed. In total contrast, God exposes in order to free us. He is the only one who has the power to fix our flaws once and for all so that we can live in joy and freedom. Ask God to reveal the flaws in yourself; he will show you his desire to remove them and fill your heart with himself. The beauty he wants to give you will never leave, and no one can ever take it away.

Too often we refuse to recognize our sin or ask God to reveal it to us. Instead, we cover up our emptiness out of fear. We smother the ache for God with a variety of distractions and lower-priority thoughts and behaviors, and the devil rejoices to see it. We numb ourselves, self-medicating vice with more vice, and the cycle of emptiness continues. The art of distraction is all about covering up what we must face if we are to move on.

Why did it take me so many years to see Jesus? My heart was deafened by the noise. I numbed myself with mind-less distractions—alcohol, relationships, parties, shopping, beauty products—you name it. I was always more interested in everybody else's life than my own, whether it was friends or celebrities in gossip magazines. I obsessed over what I looked like and what I needed to fix when it came to my body, but I avoided looking at what was broken inside. In other words, everything about my life was superficial.

And silence was my enemy. I couldn't stand silence; it made me nervous. I always had music on, was on the phone, or was texting. To get through my day, I frequently had to find new ways to distract myself. In fact, the most challenging part of a given day was those moments right before falling asleep, those silent stretches when my mind would begin to question if I was really happy—and why I wasn't. Peace was a foreign concept to me.

Believe me, I know that it is hard to sit in silence, but if we are to leave the world's messages behind and pursue God's, then sitting in silence is something we must learn. Start small. You could begin by simply not turning on the radio in your car or playing music on your phone during your daily commute. This can be uncomfortable, especially in the beginning, but carving out a space for silence is important.

Another thing you could try is starting every morning and every evening by sitting in silence. This doesn't mean you have to stare at a blank wall, but it does entail setting aside a purposeful time to engage in silence. You could look at a beautiful icon or image, perhaps a crucifix—whatever is beautiful that will invite your focus. Other times it might be helpful to meditate on a saying. I personally use the Jesus Prayer to help me begin and end my moments of silence with God: "Lord Jesus Christ, Son of God, have mercy on me, a sinner" (Mark 10:47). You can time the Jesus Prayer with your breathing to help you meditate in silence if you desire, inhaling at "Lord Jesus Christ, Son of God" and exhaling during "have mercy on me, a sinner." As far as we know, the history of the Jesus Prayer goes back to the early fifth- or sixth-century ascetic Diadochos of Photiki, who taught that repetition of the prayer leads to inner stillness.[5]

Silence is the sacred place where we hear the language of

God, and we need to learn to dwell there so we can hear his voice in our hearts. In a world full of noise, silence is a rare and undervalued gift. There are no strict rules about emptying our minds of all thoughts while we sit quietly; rather, the silence allows for God to speak to us and through our thoughts. Rather, what silence allows is for God to speak to you.

Let's revisit the story of the Samaritan woman at the well. Remember, she went at noon, when she was unlikely to meet anyone else, because she was ashamed of her lifestyle. But because she went at noon, the most silent part of the day, she encountered Jesus. Imagine if she had gone during a busy time of day; she probably would not have spoken with this random man from Nazareth. Like her, we need to set aside quiet times of the day when we can meet Christ at the well. And also just like her, we, too, are invited to leave our water jar and accept the Living Water of Christ. Commentators of the *Ignatius Catholic Study Bible* have paraphrased Augustine's insights on this, writing,

> The water jar resembles the fallen desire of man that draws pleasure from the dark wells of the world but is never satisfied for long. Conversion to Christ moves us, like the Samaritan woman, to renounce the world, leave behind the desires of our earthen vessels, and follow a new way of life.[6]

The Samaritan woman in Luke's gospel should inspire us to enter into silent contemplation with God as we ask him to help us see what is true. We must pray for an awareness of our sufferings, fears, sins—whatever is keeping us from a deeper, better relationship with him—and then ask for the courage to do something about it.

When I read about the Samaritan woman, I can feel her exhaustion from the life of sin and its weighty effects on her mind, heart, and soul—the utter fatigue from sin's slavery and isolation. Maybe she had felt the weight of this exhaustion for a very long time, but with the entrance of Christ came an activation of hope, a desire for something better than sin and regret. A desire for *more*—for the eternal, priceless love that only God offers. By getting away from the noise, she found her way to an encounter with God.

Wherever you are in your life, I invite you to gift yourself with a moment of silence right now. Calm your heart and mind. Give your worries and agendas to God. Let him hold on to them; allow your heavenly Father to calm your worries and remind you that you are his beautiful child whom he loves.

Be brave. God desires every part of us, even our chaos, hurt, concern, and fear. He sees us in full truth. He knows all of our hearts' desires, doubts, and dreams. He is the one person who knows literally everything about us and still loves us, and more than that, he has redeemed us through his Son, Jesus Christ.

Pride

The third thing that prevents us from living the life of true beauty we are called to is pride. The problem is we often don't realize when pride has found its way into how we see things. But if we are seeking true beauty, we have to take off our prideful perspective on the world and put on God's perspective. It is a difficult thing to do; the world entices us, telling us we don't need God and that we can buy our own beauty. To combat the temptation to think too much of ourselves, we must humble ourselves and seek forgiveness. In this posture of humility, we can start living for more.

When I walked out of that final photo shoot and down Fifth Avenue, my thoughts turned into extreme panic as I wondered how I was going to pay my bills and rent. What was I supposed to do now? What would I do for work? Where would I go? I tried but failed to hold back tears.

I climbed the rickety, uneven steps up to my third-floor New York apartment, got into bed, and allowed myself to fall apart. I was so tired of acting like I had my stuff together and was finally ready to put aside the attitude of pride and self-sufficiency that had pushed me to try to find my own way to beauty, love, and worth for so long.

It's hard to admit you're wrong. For years I didn't want to admit that I had made a mistake—and was continuing to make bad decisions. To admit the first one would have been to admit them all. I thought that admitting I had done something wrong would be equivalent to saying I was ugly and worthless. My pride—my inner dialogue justifying all my actions and telling me how beautiful, funny, and valuable I was—actually kept me from discovering my true value and beauty.

But at that moment, by God's grace, I finally knew I needed help, so I did what any girl would do. I called my dad.

With each unanswered ring, I felt my pride chipping away at my resolve to ask for help. It had taken all the courage I had left to dial my parents' phone number. The thought of them potentially not answering brought me to my knees in a cold sweat. What if I humbled myself and they rejected me? What would I do then? Where would I go? My eyes darted back and forth; I couldn't focus on anything. I was quickly pacing around my room when I finally heard my dad's voice say hello.

I froze, not able to respond for a few seconds.

Dad said again, "Hello?"

Then I finally answered. "Dad? . . . Dad, if you don't come and get me, I'm going to lose my soul."

There was a long pause. A very long pause. I had put it all out there in one very deep and serious statement. I had no idea what he was going to say, and then he spoke, slowly. "Okay, baby, I'm coming to get ya."

And that was it. Relief rushed into my heart. In my desperation, my pride had been vanquished. After a few more details were exchanged, I hung up the phone. The possibility that life could get better was no longer just a wish.

After my dad hung up, my mother ran upstairs, having seen that it was a New York number on the caller ID. "Was that Leah? Is she okay?"

The way my mother tells the story, my father was sitting on the edge of the bed, with one tear streaming down his face, and all he could say was this: "We got her back, Lynne. We got her back."

My mother told me that piece of the story years later. It has brought me a new awareness and appreciation of how much our parents love us, even if their love is flawed, and how deeply our lives can affect others. My parents spent the better part of those ten years, when I was between the ages of fifteen and twenty-five, praying and hoping I would return to God, realize my worth, and live a beautiful life. I never realized back then how much grief and suffering I had put my parents through, all because I wanted to live my life my way, pridefully believing my way was best.

While I waited for my dad's arrival, my pride again began to sow seeds of doubt about whether I had done the right thing. I imagined what would happen when I opened the door: the look of disappointment and the lecture detailing how I was a poor excuse of a role model for my five younger brothers and sisters, the high price my dad would have had to pay for gas to make it to New York, and the time off work he would have to take that would cancel the family's vacation time.

But I was ready for it. I was ready for whatever my dad would say to me. I would accept it. I knew whatever he had to tell me, whatever scolding I would receive, was at the bare minimum fair and just. I deserved it.

But when I opened the door, I saw something I never expected. My dad stood in the doorframe, knees bent, with a huge smile and both arms fully extended. He jumped toward me and said, "I'm so happy to see you!"

I was stunned. What in the world was going on? Didn't he know how terrible I was? I was the black sheep of the family, the screwup. Why on earth was he happy to see *me*? But my dad had dropped everything, packed so quickly that my mom had to remind him, "Patrick, you need pants! Pack pants!" and then driven two thousand miles to come get me without batting an eye. All my prideful worries were unfounded. My dad gave me a great gift that day. He showed me what forgiveness and love look like; this was what I had been missing out on all those years I'd been so trapped in my own pride.

I grabbed my keys on the counter so we could leave, but when I looked up, I saw that Dad hadn't left the doorframe. I gave him a nudging look with my eyes and said, "Come on, Dad, let's go." And I fell right into his holy little trap.

Dad held up his finger and said, "Yes, we will go. But first, first we go to confession."

"Whaat? Confession?" I stuttered.

Without skipping a beat, he added, "Leah, you called and said you wanted to come home. I am here to take you home. And Jesus is home. If you want to go anywhere else, you can call Southwest Airlines."

My parents had made each other a promise before my dad left for his road trip to pick me up. They had promised each other that, even though I had humbled myself to them, if I had no plans to humble myself and reconcile with God, then my father would kiss me on the forehead and drive all the way back home—without me. My parents knew me better than I knew myself. They knew that a new city or new home wouldn't fix my problems. They also knew that *they* couldn't fix my problems. But they did know who could, if I would set aside my pride and let him. My father understood that his job was to take me to Jesus and let Jesus do the rest.

We made our way to a randomly picked church. We didn't call ahead or make an appointment to receive the sacrament of reconciliation. I walked into the empty sanctuary alone. The lights were off, the room lit only by a small candle flickering in a red glass by the altar. I thought maybe I was in the clear and could postpone my "come to Jesus" moment a little longer. Isn't it funny how sometimes we are our own worst enemy? After everything I'd been through at this point, you'd think I would be running to Jesus, but I was still unsure and scared of allowing Christ the first place in my heart.

I decided to take a quick walk around, so as to make good on my promise to my dad and so I'd feel free to walk back out and tell him that I couldn't find a priest and that we'd just have to make our way back to St. Louis without that whole confessing-my-sins-to-Jesus thing.

As I made the obligatory walk around the sanctuary, the whole church seemed to be bursting with contemplative silence. It made me nervous. The only sounds were my feet quickly making their way toward the exit. I was just a few feet away from the main entrance when I passed by a small room to my right, the door slightly open. As I passed, I heard a man ask, "Are you there?" It scared me to death. I jumped back and, unfortunately and embarrassingly, let out a loud whispered "Noooo!"

But now I can see that it was God asking me a question

through that priest. I was so prideful and afraid to ask for God's help and his forgiveness. But in the end, God took the initiative, sidestepped my pride, and asked me, "Are you there?" God always takes the initiative, whether we realize it or not. He is always making the first gesture of love or the first invitation to return home.

As for confession, I didn't know where to begin. I couldn't possibly remember everything, but there were many sins, the worst ones, plagued my memory almost daily. The weight of regret was a burden I could no longer carry, a burden that Christ specifically asks us to give to him. It was time. I had to give Christ everything, every dark, twisted, sick little secret. It was time to stop pretending, to put my pride away, and to accept who I really was: a broken person in need of my Savior.

I walked into the confessional room and knelt down at the kneeler. A crucifix hung above, depicting the ultimate example of beauty letting go of pride, and I proceeded to tell the priest that it had been almost a decade since I had reconciled myself with the Lord. I admitted to forgetting some of the prayers and really didn't know where to begin. The priest was incredibly kind. He immediately reminded me that it was *Jesus*, not him, who would hear and forgive my sins; it was *Jesus* who died for me; and it was *Jesus* who would give me love and, ultimately, peace. He suggested that I first confess the sin that I was most afraid to share, the one that brought with it the most shame and regret. At first I thought this was a great idea. Say the worst one first, get it out of the way, and make my way down the list. I asked for a minute to think through things; I had a lot of first-place contenders. He told me to take my time. My mind was racing.

Eventually, I regained my composure and said I was ready to begin. With a deep, choppy inhale and exhale, I confessed the sin that had brought me the worst pain, regret, and shame. In that moment I crushed my pride.

The priest gently said, "Very good. Remember you are speaking to Christ, so give Christ your second-worst offense."

And with that I confessed the second one.

Just one more time, the priest leaned into the screen and, with a slight stutter, said, "O-okay. So, I think maybe you should have said the second one first."

I couldn't help but laugh. I thought I knew so much, but I didn't even know which of my sins to call the worst! I didn't know what true beauty was, so how could I know degrees of ugliness? That bit of laughter allowed me to relax a bit and continue on.

As I confessed my sins, hearing them aloud was surreal. What my lips said and ears heard was a powerful dose of reality. I confessed the worst of me: the longing for love and beauty and the ways I tried to satisfy those desires with the world. I confessed my role in leading others away from what was true and good. I confessed my doubt in God's love. I confessed every single piece of brokenness, every ounce of regret.

I gave God my pride and my sins, and God gave me his merciful love. As the priest prayed over me after I had finished, he ended with this blessing: "Go in peace, and proclaim to the world the wonderful works of God who has brought you salvation." Another way of phrasing that final prayer is "Go be a reflection of God's glory in the world. Be beautiful."

I walked out of that confessional believing and feeling like a new creation in Christ. I had let go of the exhausting burden of being, in essence, my own god, and now I knew I was forgiven by the only true God. My pride had been defeated. Now a new life in Christ awaited me: one that embraced God's plan for true beauty and love rather than my own.

I particularly love the scripture Matthew 11:28, where Jesus says, "Come to me, all you who are weary and burdened, and I will give you rest" (NIV). It meant even more to me when I found out my name, Leah, means "the weary." Within my own namesake lay the call to put down the burden of pride and rest my labors upon Christ.

You may not have gone as far away from God as I did. Your life might not have been as lacking in beauty as mine was at that time. But I know that at one time or another, we all forget our identities as sons and daughters of God. We all drift away from true beauty and forget our worth. So, for all of us, asking for forgiveness is an essential virtue.

Thankfully, there is no inquisition and no defense we must give as to why we are worthy of forgiveness. We are worthy not because of anything we did, but simply because we are God's sons and daughters. If God's approach to us was based on our actions rather than on our child-parent relationship with him, he would give us what we deserve: nothing. The fact that we are owed nothing is why God's act of forgiveness is truly an act of love. He forgives not because he has to but because he loves us and desires for us to be reunited with him through Christ. We don't have to earn it; we just have to accept the gift that God holds out to us. God's love, which is undeserved, invaluable, and overwhelming, stands in vast contrast to the false love and imitation beauty the world offers.

There is no question. God *will* forgive our sins *if* we ask him to. Pope Francis said, "God never tires of forgiving us; we are the ones who tire of seeking his mercy."[7] God's only requirement is a contrite heart that humbly submits to truth and love. As the psalmist says in Scripture,

> For you do not desire sacrifice, or else I would give it;
> You do not delight in burnt offering.
> The sacrifices of God are a broken spirit;
> A broken and contrite heart—
> These, O God, You will not despise."
>
> (Ps. 51:16–17 NKJV).

The first step in taking on God's perspective of beauty is quite simple. Lay aside your pride and ask. Sometimes the easiest way out of the darkness is walking in a straight line toward the light.

Doubt

Once we've gotten past our fear, the noise of the world, and our pride, and started on the path toward the life of beauty

God made us for, we may feel we're in good shape. The truth is, though, we might still find ourselves stumbling a bit and suddenly facing a battle with the fourth thing that tries to hold us back—doubt. Even after my dad drove two thousand miles to knock on my door and bring me home, at times I still found myself flooded with memories of my past life. I experienced flashbacks of my actions, my sins, my regrets, and my feelings of unworthiness and utter disgust with myself. My memories would tempt me to doubt God's love and even foster hesitation in me about accepting the new life Christ offered.

Even though I'd been forgiven and made new, I felt a strong temptation to identify with my old sins, to see myself as bad because of my past full of wrong choices, with no one else to blame but myself. But that's what the evil one wants us to believe, that we *are* our sins. The evil one wants us to think, live, and act as if we are damaged goods, ugly and worthless. This. Is. A. Lie. We must not believe it, and if we hear it, we must banish those thoughts straight to hell where they belong.

Notice how similar those same doubtful, self-defeating thoughts are to the ones the beauty industry tries to make us believe: we may have lots of flaws, but if we're willing to pay the price, we could fix them. We could be prettier, so we should buy some concealer. Everyone will know at a glance how much we're worth by what we're wearing, so we should buy lots of expensive clothes. The ugly truth at the bottom of these pretty lies is that the world is saying we are not enough, and never will be, so we had better pile on and wrap ourselves in whatever the beauty industry is selling.

These labels the world gives us, the ones Satan whispers to us as we're trying to pursue God's path, are lies. Satan may call us by our sins, but God calls us by our names, the people he created us to be—his sons and daughters. And as we learn to stand firm in our God-given names, we begin to act like the sons and daughters of God that we are. It is a process, though. The loving work of Christ to make us new beautiful creations is not a one-and-done experience. It's a journey that unfolds more of his love for us with each passing day.

You see, I believe in the love of Jesus Christ. I believe in his words, and I know he will not fail us (Heb. 13:5), he will not forsake us (Deut. 31:6), and he will make good on his promises (Jer. 29:11). But, regardless of *knowing* this, *feeling* this can still be difficult at times. Our hesitant surrender to embrace a life of beauty is often a symptom of us doubting God's incredible love for us. To overcome that doubt, the strongest defense is Holy Scripture.

So as I began walking this bumpy road toward the One who is beauty, truth, and love, I steeped myself in Scripture, focusing on a few verses in particular that spoke to my identity. If I ever began to question God's mercy to me, my mind would immediately go to these verses and smash the doubts. The antidote to doubt is to remember who you really are.

One particular passage that has spoken deeply to me is the parable of the prodigal son, found in Luke 15. The parallel between that story and my own is more than clear. Let's look at the end of the parable, when the son finally repents of his worldly ways:

> And he arose and came to his father. But while he was yet at a distance, his father saw him and had compassion, and ran and embraced him and kissed him. And the son said to him, "Father, I have sinned against heaven and before you; I am no longer worthy to be called your son." But the father said to his servants, "Bring quickly the best robe, and put it on him; and put a ring on his hand, and shoes on his feet; and bring the fatted calf and kill it, and let us eat and make merry; for this my son was dead, and is alive again; he was lost, and is found." And they began to make merry. (Luke 15:20–24)

You're probably familiar with this story, but oftentimes we miss the smaller details that bring more depth to its meaning. For many of us sinners this parable hits home, and many books have been written to try to capture all the meaning found within it. However, a few key points always remain with me when I ponder what it is to embrace the love of Christ and pursue a life of true beauty.

Identity. The parable begins as the prodigal son asks his father for his inheritance. This is not the same as a kid today asking their wealthy dad for more moola in their trust fund. An inheritance is what a child gets only after his dad dies. It is part of the child's identity, his connection to his family. The prodigal son is basically saying, "I don't want to be in a relationship with you. I wish you were dead. So can I have my share now?" This would have to hurt the father more than the sinful life the son led afterward. It is a rejection of the son's very identity as the father's child.

How often have we taken the blessings from God without gratitude or thanksgiving and lived as if God did not exist at all? Instead, we used his gifts—our lives, our health, our relationships—for our own selfish or disordered desires and rejected the very relationship that gives us our identity. Even if we say that we believe there is a God, do we act as if there is a God?[8] Our actions reveal what we truly believe.

Yet, our identity as daughters of God that is the foundation of our worth. Our family relationship to God and to one another gives our lives meaning and value. If we reject our identity, as the prodigal son did, I am certain there is nothing down that path but loneliness and despair.

A far country. Despite this great insult, the father gives his son his inheritance, and the son departs for some crazy loose living in a far country. A "far country" means that he left his home in the Holy Land and lived among pagans and Gentiles, where his actions would not be questioned.

Sinning is easier when we are not held accountable by our family and good friends. This scripture convicts me when I think of my past life. Living a life void of God was easier when I surrounded myself with others who didn't care about tomorrow, consequences, or my soul.

Once again, leaving for a far country is a question of identity: Where is your home? Where is your family? As

Christians we know our eternal home is in heaven with God, and we make our earthly home with our church communities and among those whose values we share. A far country for us can equate to not going to church for some time or even something as simple as avoiding conversations with our family members. We don't have to go to Europe to become like the prodigal son.

At a distance. Now we get to the best part. Look again at what Luke 15:20 says: "But while he was yet at a distance, his father saw him and had compassion, and ran and embraced him and kissed him."

Nothing warms my heart more than this line. With his apology rehearsed, the son returns home after squandering his father's inheritance, and his father sees him coming at a distance. His father has been *waiting* for him. Waiting for his return. God the Father waits for us to turn our hearts back to him. And when the son comes back, the father restores his sonship, just as God does for us through Jesus Christ. Before the son can even get out his fully rehearsed apology, the father has already forgiven him.

Even if we forget or reject our identity, God does not. He never forgets you. He never forgets that you are his daughter, and he will never reject you when you return home to him. At the end of the parable, the father gives the son the best robe in the house and puts a ring on his finger and sandals on his feet. These are all signs of his restored identity as the father's son with all the rights and possessions that come with that identity.

The Lord loves the lost, and the Lord seeks out the lost. Why? He desires to be unified with you. He desires true beauty to be resident in your soul. If you've come to realize that you haven't been walking in the beauty God calls you to, as I did all those years ago, take heart. Don't give in to doubt. Remember your identity, and come home.

6

BECOMING BEAUTIFUL

DESIRING TO BE BEAUTIFUL ACCORDING TO God's definition is the first step toward living a beautiful life. But we don't get to the finish line by just wanting something. With God's grace, we must do more to become beautiful, as I learned in those early days after I returned home. Beyond asking for and accepting the forgiveness of Christ, the battle over the day-to-day practical living with Christ, with beauty, was just beginning. I knew that now life *had* to be different. It could not possibly stay the same, nor did I want it to.

We cannot expect different results from our lives if we do nothing to change them. If we want a better life, then something has to shift. We are called to ask for and then act on God's love and mercy for us. Receiving Christ's love compels us to change, to become an example of his grace for the glory of God and for others.

So, when I returned home, I knew I needed to change.

I started with reaching for a better definition of love and beauty, because how we act flows from who we are, and who we are is largely determined by how we understand the world. Changing my habits started first with changing my terms. I had been living according to the false idea that love was doing whatever led to me feeling valued, and beauty, defined as just looking good, was a means to obtaining that. I had been brainwashed by secular culture to believe my exterior beauty *was* the sum total of my worth and identity. Being made new again in Christ meant letting go of the world's idea of beauty once and for all.

Beyond changing my terms, I needed a plan of action if I was really going to live a life of holiness and virtue. Previously I had never had a game plan of what to do or even a basic list of what not to do. I simply did whatever felt good and either tried to ignore any consequences or just deal with them as they came. Now it was clear that I needed an actual plan for my life; I wanted to be purposeful in living a truly beautiful one. I wanted to place doing good above and beyond the desire of looking good. I wanted my life to reflect Jesus, who is the source and summit of beauty.

Embracing the Beauty of Chastity

Some actions changed immediately, in particular regarding my dating life. Since I no longer viewed my body as a tool or an object to be used but rather as a "temple of the Holy Spirit"

(1 Cor. 6:19), I knew I needed to take up the virtue of chastity, which "lets us love with an upright and undivided heart."[1] I needed to recommit myself to a life in which I lived out my value as a daughter of God, and that started with treating my body and my relationships with the dignity they deserved.

Chastity is often misunderstood as a disdain for the body or for sex. Or it is misunderstood as a sort of twisted repression of desire. On the contrary, chastity loves and respects the body, and it purifies desire rather than repressing it. Chastity is not just for those who take vows of celibacy; chastity is for single and even married people!

> The virtue of chastity [. . .] is for everyone. Chastity is not about saying "no" to sex. Chastity is about saying "yes" to God's plan for our sexuality. No matter where he is in his life, a chaste person masters his sexual feelings, and knows how to express them at the proper times.[2]

Chastity is an important virtue because it frees love from the utilitarian attitude of use. It includes an "apprenticeship in self-mastery, which is a training in human freedom. The alternative is clear: either man governs his passions and finds peace, or he lets himself be dominated by them and becomes unhappy."[3] Self-mastery of my emotions and passions was the total opposite of my old habits where I actively sought to please my emotions and passions. It's not easy, but it is possible, and, more importantly, it respects a person's inherent worth. Even a married person, out of love for the other spouse, can't engage in sexual activity whenever he or she desires. Marriage is not license to let your desires run wild. The virtue of chastity in marriage means that you will make decisions about sexual activity with your spouse in mind, not merely to fulfill your desires. I may have lost my virginity years ago, but with God's grace I could regain my purity.

And so I vowed to never give myself away again. No matter how many "I love yous" were heard or said, I was not going to share the gift of my body with someone who was not 100 percent committed to me. I was looking for the type of commitment that requires a man to stand in front of all of my family and friends and God himself and vow to love me until death. That's the type of commitment I was worth. That's the type of commitment you are worth.

Embracing the Beauty of Holiness

Every single one of us is called to live a beautiful life. But, as we know by now, that doesn't mean we are all called to be runway models. If we had to sum up with one word what a life of beauty looks like, it would be *holiness*. What does that mean? Holiness isn't a very popular word since it is often used to describe "holier-than-thou" sorts of people. But holiness basically means "like God." If we are holy to any degree, we are like God. And since God is the embodiment of love and beauty, holiness is a life where we are single-mindedly in pursuit of love and beauty, of God himself. While our paths to holiness may all look different, the call of every Christian is the call to holiness.[4] Beauty rooted in holiness will never fade. While our physical appearance may lose its luster from our younger years, the beauty of holiness has the potential of growing more brilliant with age.

My particular path to embracing a beautiful life had to begin with addressing the uncomfortable reality that I had never asked God what *he* wanted for me. I was always too afraid God's plans would leave me unhappy or unloved, with no value in the eyes of the world. I see now how absurd this is, but back then fear controlled a lot of my life. When I realized that God actually *wants* my happiness—that he wants me to know, experience, and share authentic love, and ultimately desires for me to live a life of true beauty—it became easier to offer my days and my choices to him.

We are told from a young age that we can be whatever we want to be, both now and when we grow up. The emphasis is on you, as in "*you* need to search deep within to discover what *you* want." But the Christian view is radically different. Instead of looking to ourselves for the answer, we look to God. When we look to God to answer the question of what our life's work will be, he reveals what he has planned for our lives, as he says in Jeremiah 29:11: "'For I know the plans I have for you,' declares the LORD" (NIV). And God's plan is always more beautiful than our plans. Once again, this is the Christian difference. A life of beauty and holiness isn't centered on us but rather is centered on God and others.

Asking God what his plans were for me was an incredibly

vulnerable experience. I began a habit of asking God what his will was for me throughout my day. This helped me keep my day and to-do list in check and continually reminded me that I was not alone. Beyond these day-to-day check-ins with God, I knew I also had to ask him what he desired for my life overall. Was he calling me to devote my life to full-time ministry? Was he calling me to the specific ministry of marriage and motherhood? I ended up spending three years asking God what path he had for me. During that time, I visited different orders, like the Missionaries of Charity, journaled, spoke with my spiritual director, and kept up a consistent prayer life.

As we turn away from what the world tells us we should do and instead seek how God wants each of us to live a life of beauty, we need not be afraid. God's will for us brings peace, freedom, and joy, and so even if his plan ends up being a path we had not considered, the response we'll have in our hearts when it becomes clear is a free and total yes. For me, after all my seeking, I discovered God was calling me to pursue my path to holiness through marriage. Even though I didn't get married until five years later, God gave me the peace of knowing the path he had planned for me.

Will you give up your own plans and the path the world would push you toward to pursue God's plan for your life? Let's look at the stories of a few more women who courageously chose to invite God into their plans and embrace a life of true beauty.

The successful Spanish actress and model Olalla Oliveros starred in movies and advertisements around the world before having what she called an "earthquake experience" of encountering Christ. Following a pilgrimage visit to Fátima, Portugal, she says she received in her mind the image of herself dressed as nun, something she said she initially found absurd. However, she couldn't get the image out of her head and eventually concluded that Jesus was calling her to give up her glamorous life and become a nun. "The Lord is never wrong," she said. "He asked if I will follow him, and I could not refuse."[5] She is now a member of the semicloistered Order of Saint Michael.

Amada Rosa Pérez was one of Colombia's top models but disappeared from the public eye for a period of five years due to being diagnosed with a disease that left her with only 60 percent of her hearing in her left ear. This caused her to question her lifestyle. "I felt disappointed, unsatisfied, directionless, submerged in fleeting pleasures," she said. "I always sought answers and the world never gave them to me." While Amada admits to being open to religious life, she felt God calling her to marriage and children. She now works tirelessly with a Marian religious community in Colombia. She also has reevaluated what it means to be a fashion model: "Before I was always in a hurry, stressed out, and got upset easily," she continued. "Now I live in peace, the world doesn't appeal to me. I enjoy every moment the Lord gives me."[6]

Many other women have left the empty promises of the world to pursue a beautiful life with God. Kylie Bisutti won the Victoria's Secret Model Search and was on her way to becoming an "Angel" for the lingerie giant until she found God, causing a media whirlwind on Twitter with this tweet:

"I stopped being a Victoria [*sic*] Secret model to become a Proverbs 31 wife!"[7]

Nicole Weider was a former model who struggled with depression, thoughts of suicide, and body-image issues. She admits, "Through my modeling jobs, I started developing anxiety, and each time a camera was focused on me, I didn't feel skinny enough, pretty enough, or completely ready to be scrutinized by the people who make it all happen. I tried to hide it and forget about my problems by going to the hottest clubs, partying and drinking with celebrities, yet I still felt lost. I needed God badly in my life."[8] She has since abandoned the world's call to follow God's. She now is the founder of Project Inspired, a website for teen girls that analyzes pop culture and explores ways girls can live in their authentic beauty.

God can do so much in our lives if we let him. It all begins with first looking to God for our identity, worth, and plans. Invite God into your life. Ask him what he wants for you. As Pope John Paul II wisely said, "True living is not found in one's self or in things. It is found in Someone else, in the One who created everything that is good, true, and beautiful in the world."[9] Too many young women look to the world for their identity, worth, and true calling. Too many spend countless hours filling their heads and hearts with distorted ideas about beauty and love that only result in over-sexualization and objectification for women, all in the name of freedom and feminism.

A beautiful life is one that takes its lead from God, not *Cosmopolitan*, Tiffany & Co., Manolo Blahnik, or any other fashion influence. A beautiful life is one that gives God permission to fill our hearts and heads, to inspire us, influence us, and change us for the better.

God has a plan for you. God knows you and loves exactly who you are, wherever you are, *right now*. But he wants more for you than you want for yourself. He desires to give you more. I urge you to take Pope John Paul II's words to heart: "Have the courage to commit yourselves to the truth. Have the courage to believe the good news about life which Jesus teaches in the Gospel. Open your minds and hearts to the beauty of all God has made and to his special, personal love for each one of you."[10] Have the courage to trust our loving, beautiful Savior with yourself, your life.

7

SHARING BEAUTY

MY FIRST TIME VISITING THE SISTINE CHAPEL, I stood in complete awe of Michelangelo's work. I stared for what felt like days, jaw dropped at such magnificent talent, dedication, perseverance, and beauty. When my eyes came to the scene of creation painted on the ceiling, with God touching the finger of Adam and thus pouring life into him, I noticed something to the right of the image of God. Actually, it wasn't just something; it was someone. It was Eve! Michelangelo had painted her under the arm of God, in heaven, while he gave life to Adam in his soul.

I was ecstatic! Too often Eve gets a bad rap—I get it; I understand why—but here on the ceiling of the Sistine Chapel I witnessed a beautiful Eve. She was strong; she looked like she knew her beauty, her dignity, and her identity. She had her arm wrapped around God's arm. It was the most powerful painting I had personally ever seen, and I felt in that moment that I just had to tell someone about it. I yelled, "It's Eve! Look! It's Eve!"

Just so you know, when you walk into the heavily guarded Sistine Chapel, there are rules, such as no photography and the mandate of silence. But I couldn't help myself with my outburst. Seeing Eve—how she was painted, where Michelangelo had placed her—was amazingly beautiful to me. It was innocent Eve, Eve before sin. It was all the best of her, and Michelangelo painted her strong, beautiful, and trusting of God—Eve content and fulfilled. This is how we were made to be: strong and confident, brave and beautiful, but still trustingly dependent on God the Father. Staring at the strong grip Eve had on God's arm, I began to reflect on how many times I had held on tightly to the wrong men and placed my trust in them instead of God.

I felt compelled to shout, to share the beauty of Eve, because when we encounter authentic beauty—beauty that reflects the glory of God in the world—it by its nature pushes us toward others. In contrast, the disordered, self-seeking beauty of the world turns our bodies into idols. It is ultimately the worship of self. This self-worship is isolating and traps us, sometimes without us realizing it, into a life of individualism, where we think only of ourselves rather than of others:

> Too often, though, the beauty that is thrust upon us is illusory and deceitful, superficial and blinding, leaving the onlooker dazed; instead of bringing him out of himself and opening him up to horizons of true freedom as it draws

him aloft, it imprisons him within himself and further enslaves him, depriving him of hope and joy. It is a seductive but hypocritical beauty that rekindles desire, the will to power, to possess, and to dominate others, it is a beauty which soon turns into its opposite, taking on the guise of indecency, transgression or gratuitous provocation.[1]

Not only does disordered beauty imprison us in loneliness, it actually leads us to dominate others and ultimately to treat them below their dignity. So it has a consequence both for us and for society.

Choosing God's true beauty, on the other hand, leads to a life that is the opposite of isolated and purely individualistic. When we choose true beauty, we are necessarily choosing God since he embodies truth and beauty. And when we embrace that beauty, our hearts align with God's heart, which is always for other people. God's mission on earth is to form a community of love among his people. Unlike the inward, selfish focus of imitation beauty, authentic beauty turns us outward and makes us concerned with the needs of others.

To quote the poet John Donne, "no man is an island." Human beings do not thrive when isolated from others. Why else would solitary confinement be a punishment in prisons? We are created to be in communion with one another. Not only that, but we all affect one another. Therefore, how we live and what we do matters more than we might think, because our choices—even when they seem to be personal or private choices—influence others as well. So rather than walk in the inwardly focused way of imitation beauty, let's decide that our lives will be expressions of authentic beauty that point outward and, ultimately, back to God.

I believe we women are specially called to be the guardians and ambassadors of beauty. After all, we are the ones who are relentlessly targeted by advertisements to buy products that, in the end, only obscure our dignity and detract from our purpose. Therefore, it should be us who reclaim beauty and remind the world that we are more than a collection of parts, that beauty is beyond the physical, and our value, worth, and identity are not based on any ideas created by a marketing agency but on the word of the Almighty. Beauty belongs to God, not the world. Archbishop Fulton Sheen, a great social commentator, said,

> To a great extent the level of any civilization is the level of its womanhood. When a man loves a woman, he has to become worthy of her. The higher her virtue, the more noble her character, the more devoted she is to truth, justice, and goodness, the more a man has to aspire to be worthy of her. The history of civilization could actually be written in terms of the level of its women.[2]

Women give life to civilization both literally and figuratively. Literally, because without women, there would be no children, and figuratively because women are especially capable of setting the bar for dignity and beauty in a culture. Let us share beauty with the world in every aspect of our being.

Beauty in Dress

Embracing God's definition of beauty is liberating, but how do we live it out practically? Of the many virtues that can help us lead authentically beautiful lives, we should start with one in particular. A fantastically underrated virtue and champion for beauty is modesty. For most of us, the word *modesty* reminds us of a school principal wagging her finger in disapproval of painted nails or a too-short skirt or, God forbid, a bare shoulder.

In the grand scheme of things, no part of the body is inherently bad or sinful. Your body is good. All of it. It is not out of shame that we cover some parts of ourselves. Rather, it is because our body is good that we need to keep some parts covered or protected. Those parts of our bodies with a sexual value attached to them require more protection so that they are not on display at inappropriate times.

Believe it or not, modesty is not the bane of beauty but its ambassador. Modesty is about the spiritual dignity proper to humans.[3] It is an awakening in our conscience to respect the human person, which includes ourselves and others. It guides how we look at others and behave toward them.[4] It protects the intimate center of the person and refuses to unveil what should remain hidden.[5] This is not an oppressive or restrictive standard. On the contrary, with these purposes in mind, we start to see that modesty is a protector, a defender of our bodies whose goal is our dignity.

Contrary to popular thought, modesty does not just apply

to what we wear. Modesty in all its facets—in our speech, in our dress, and in our actions—matters. It matters because we matter, and we interact with other humans on this great planet, and *they* matter too!

While it is true that beauty is so much more than our physical selves, that doesn't mean we shouldn't care about how we look. Our outward appearance should reflect our heart, our interior self. While Coco Chanel, Ralph Lauren, and Calvin Klein are some of the most famous fashion houses in history, the award for first fashion designer actually goes to someone else.

In Genesis 3:21 we read, "And the LORD God made for Adam and for his wife garments of skin, and clothed them." Here we have biblical evidence that God was the very first fashion designer! It is important to note that this action from God came after Adam and Eve attempted to clothe themselves with fig leaves and hid in the garden of Eden. It's not that Adam and Eve were completely naked and needed clothes; they had already clothed themselves as best as they could. But somehow those man-made clothes were inadequate, for they hid and did not present themselves to each other or to God. So God made them new clothes, that is, clothing adequate to their dignity.

The truth is that God *does* care about what we wear. Not in terms of size, color, or designer, but in terms of our bodies being veiled, or clothed, appropriate to our dignity. If someone loves you totally in mind, body, and soul, he or she is going to care about everything that affects you in mind, body, and soul. Perhaps you've experienced that kind of care from your family, but God's care extends so much further than we can imagine; it encompasses everything that affects us, every choice we make—our entire being. So if you think that God doesn't care about what we wear, then you've missed the lesson from Genesis. God loves us and wants our greatest happiness and our greatest dignity, even when we don't want it for ourselves.

Sometimes what we say in response to the call for modesty is some version of "I should be able to wear whatever I want, whenever I want," but this doesn't really hold up when put to the test. Our clothing sends messages, but not just negative messages; our clothing can also send messages of respect. Those with the most money and the most power to choose what to wear know this.

When the Duke and Duchess of Cambridge—or William and Kate—visited India, Kate chose more modest clothing to match the occasion and the culture. For their meeting with the Indian prime minister, Narendra Modi, Kate had her dress tailored to include a modesty panel in the front to cover her décolletage. The original dress had featured a lace panel running down the top, which would have required her to go braless, and long panels of see-through lace on the skirt would have revealed a good portion of her upper thighs.[6] Her choice showed self-awareness and respect for another person's culture and customs, for their dignity as well as her own. Kate clearly understands the art of fashion and modesty.

Clothing, or lack of clothing, is a powerful communicator.

Recent studies support the common sense notion that what we wear can have an effect on what others think of us. One study found that showing men pictures of sexualized women stirs up less activity in areas of the brain that are normally activated when we look at a person who we think is capable of thought and planned action. When these men were shown full-body shots of women as compared to face shots, they judged the women in the full-body shots to be less intelligent, less likable, less ambitious, and less competent.[7] The reality is that the psychology of males and females is just different; women tend to be more verbal and men more visual.[8] Knowing that, we should assist our partners through our choice of dress whenever possible.

And to be fair, how we dress affects us too. "Clothing represents an important contributor to the body and emotional experience of contemporary young women" because clothing that only highlights parts of a woman leads to increased self-objectification, body shame, body dissatisfaction, and negative mood.[9]

Our oversexualized culture is affecting everyone, even children. Studies show that girls as young as six years old are sexualizing themselves because the messages in media show sexiness as something that is rewarded.[10] The American Psychological Association reports that "massive exposure to media among youth creates the potential for massive exposure to portrayals that sexualize women and girls and teach girls that women are sexual objects."[11] Fashion magazines are giving advice to young girls and women on how to look and dress to attract men, therefore encouraging "young women to think of themselves as sexual objects whose lives are not complete unless sexually connected with a man."[12]

Modesty requires bravery because it is so countercultural. We need to show the world that we are not a collection of body parts but whole women with dignity, purpose, and power. We can do this by taking it one step further and cultivating an interior disposition toward beauty that affects not only our clothing choices but also our actions and thoughts. If beauty is what delights the soul upon being known, then modesty is beauty's first line of defense. Modesty celebrates and defends the integrated, proportionate, and clear vision of beauty in every living thing and person.

So how do we take all this into account and live it out on a practical level? God respects our free will, our different bodies, and our unique tastes. So, while God does not give us a dress code, he does exhort us to use common sense. Remember, he came to save us from our sins, not our brains, so it's a good idea to use them.

Atmospheres, occasions, and weather can dictate our attire as we consider what is appropriate, but how do we know if our outfit is modest or not, and whether it is in line with our understanding of beauty? A good rule of thumb is this: Modest fashion should highlight the whole person, not just parts of a person. It is not just about a hemline or an effort to hide our bodies; it's a virtue that helps us reveal our dignity.

In the appendix are some basic guidelines[13] I try to live by. These guidelines are my own; they are not private revelations from Jesus. Feel free to disagree with them or adapt them to your needs, but in your pursuit of modesty make sure that your fashions do not compromise the dignity of the human person or create opportunities for objectification. I pray these guidelines help you achieve freedom in fashion and help you live out your beauty in wholeness and holiness.[14]

While on the red carpet for the finale of *America's Next Top Model*, we were told to memorize the names of the designers for everything we were wearing, from earrings to dresses to shoes. It was imperative that we got the correct pronunciation, and we even rehearsed with the stylists and some of the judges just to be sure *they* were not embarrassed by our lack of fashion expertise.

Sure enough, as soon as I hit the red carpet a multitude of paparazzi began taking pictures, asking repeatedly, "Who are you wearing?" It seemed this was all they cared about. And I get it; that's the fashion business. But even after my conversion, that question, "Who are you wearing?" has stuck with me. Our fashions that we wear every day may not say outright that we love Jesus, but there are definitely some outfits that say we don't care about Jesus. My past fashions certainly did not convey that I was a believer. If anything, my fashions back then revealed that I belonged to the world.

After dedicating my life back to Christ, I had to make a lot of changes. However, the last change I made was to my wardrobe. It was painfully obvious that my outward expression needed to match what was going on in my head and heart. It didn't make any sense for me to continue wearing backless or *very* low V-necked tops with miniskirts to my new women's Bible study group. I had to be all-in or not in at all, and so I asked myself that same question I had heard years before: "Leah, who are you wearing?" My old clothes were telling a story I didn't believe in anymore. It was time for a change. It was time for Christ.

Who are you wearing? Are you wearing the world, or are you wearing Christ?

Beauty in Action

Modest dress is one excellent way to practice living out a beautiful life, but if we stop there, we have allowed our modest fashions to become a type of costume that we can put on and take off at will. Choosing to dress modestly should be an indication to others that our actions and speech will also be ordered by holiness.

Action follows being; in other words, what we do flows from who we are. The internal conversion of the heart and mind is what affects everything else: our thinking, dress, speech, and actions. These, in turn, affect other people. Beauty's highest calling, its mission, is to draw others to God. Beauty serves as a pathway to the divine love of Jesus, which inspires and empowers all things for good. Because beauty offers the world a real encounter with God, everything we do should be in line with this mission.

One of the most beautiful women I have never met is

Mother Teresa of Calcutta, now Saint Mother Teresa. I was in Rome for her canonization and could not believe how many people of all different types of religion, and some with none at all, came to celebrate the life of a woman who loved and cared for others. In the back of St. Peter's Square I was wedged between a group of Buddhists and a group of agnostics. Our eyes were glued to the big screens that the Vatican had put up for the growing crowds. Together we watched Pope Francis speak of Mother Teresa's life and legacy of beauty and love. And together we all clapped, cried, and cheered upon hearing the words "Santa Teresa!"

During her life, Mother Teresa was one of the most photographed women in the world. The world was attracted to her and admired her for her Christian service. As I discussed in chapter 4, Mother Teresa's authentic beauty flowed out of her love for others, and her life was a living expression of the love of Jesus to everyone she met. One of my favorite stories about her was a time when she was taking care of a Hindu man who was abandoned and whose body was half eaten away by worms and maggots.

As Mother Teresa was taking care of the man, he asked her, "Why are you doing this for me? Everyone else has thrown me away."

She replied, "I love you; you are Jesus in the distressing disguise. Jesus is sharing his passion with you."

The Hindu man then said, "Glory be to Jesus Christ!" The Hindu praised Jesus because of how Mother Teresa loved him and displayed God's glory, his beauty, in action.[15]

Beauty in action is wonderfully attractive. It makes others pause and notice. It forces one to ask, "How is she like that?" Ultimately, the answer to that question will point to God because without him we don't have the strength to do beautiful things.

There are many kinds of beautiful actions. Let's talk about five kinds that have been particularly powerful in my own life.

Beauty in Friendship

Kim was diagnosed with a brain tumor. After having surgery, she had to begin six weeks of radiation and, being a school teacher, she had to schedule her radiation before the school day began. Kim's alarm went off every morning at 5:00, and she left her house at 5:45 to make her way into Pittsburgh, Pennsylvania, for her radiation treatment scheduled for 6:45 a.m. After radiation, Kim rushed to school to arrive by 8:00 every day. On the first few days, she would get a text at 5:15 a.m. from her friend Laura. It would be some sort of inspirational rhyme, such as "It's day one, but do not fear. You can do this, your God is here!"

About three days in, Kim finally texted her back and said, "Why are you up every morning at 5:15 a.m.?"

Laura responded, "Because you are. I can't do much for you for the next six weeks since I am in North Carolina, but I can get up at the same time as you to support you and pray for you."

Kim was blown away and admitted, "The selflessness of

that act has never left my heart. I have never had a friend do anything like that for me before. Laura showed me the true meaning of friendship, and I will never forget that."

Laura's act of friendship, waking every morning with her suffering friend, is beautiful. It recognized the truth of her friend's suffering; it did not ignore it or make light of it. And in response to that truth, Laura's heart flowered in love for her friend and inspired her to do this beautiful act. Kim could not believe it but had to ask, "Why is it that you do this?"

Beauty in friendship is one of the most important ways we can draw others to God. Much of each day is spent interacting with other people, so if we make our relationships beautiful, they can impact the world.

In our culture, we struggle with friendship. We live in an individualistic culture where we primarily look out for ourselves and spend the majority of our time on ourselves. In contrast to that mind-set, friendship that seeks the good of the other is a way of sharing beauty with others. My husband, Ricky, often says, "You're the average of the five people around you." I wish I had heard that line when I was in high school, college, or when I was floundering in New York. If I was the average of my friends during my days in New York, my number was pretty dang low. And to be fair, I wasn't helping to bring up the average either.

The friends from my past were people who participated in the same party-style atmosphere I had grown accustomed to. Our interactions revolved around what party we were going to next, who was dating who, what job people had and how much money they made, and so on. It was all quite superficial and rooted in consumerism, materialism, and hedonism, not beauty. No one, and I mean no one, spoke of Christ or God or faith. If it was ever brought up, people whispered it, as if it were a curse word. I called these people my friends. Clearly, I had no idea what a beautiful friend looked like, and I sure as heck didn't know how to act like one.

In fact, when my dad came to pick me up from New York, I moved out of my apartment without talking to my room-mates. One of the girls was in Milan modeling, and the other was always at her boyfriend's house in Queens. I did not leave a note, did not call, nothing; I just left. And to my shock no one called me, no one asked where I was, no one came won-dering if I was going to pay my share of the rent or utilities. I could have been dead in a gutter and no one would have cared to search for me. These were the type of "friends" I had back then—everyone out for themselves, everyone turned inward.

Whom we allow into our lives matters more than we might think. These friends can influence some of our big-gest and most important life choices. This is why, ideally, we want to cultivate friendships with people who not only share similar interests but are also smarter, holier, and more beau-tiful, in the best sense, than we are. Not only will these types of people challenge us and keep us accountable, but they'll hopefully bring up our average by helping us become smarter, holier, and better.

Proverbs 27:17 wisely says, "As iron sharpens iron, so one person sharpens another" (NIV). True friends speak truth to you, make you better, and challenge you. True friends know they can't complete you or make you happy, but they aid and guide you to the One who does.

Choosing better friends and letting go of the old ones was one of my first battles in my new life of beauty. After walking away from my old friends, I realized I did not have one single true friend left from my past. For all of my young adult life, I had depended on other people like a crutch to give me value and make me feel loved. I used friendships to distract me from the growing needs of my heart and to avoid loneliness. Letting go of everyone who had previously kept me down was strangely liberating, but it also made me feel very lonely. But in prayer I could hear Jesus tell me, "I'm your friend. I am enough." When I allowed Christ to enter my life, he gave me this alone time so that I would learn to embrace the truth that he *was* enough for me. I needed to learn this lesson: before filling up my life with any other relationship, I must first allow Christ to fill me and teach me what true friendship looks like.

Being alone and being lonely are two different things, and in our search for beautiful friendship, knowing the difference is important. We all have moments when we feel lonely, some of us more than others. Loneliness can bring isolation, and sometimes fear of rejection as well. We often search for something to fill the ache and assure us of our identity when we're feeling lonely. But this should not be confused with being alone. We are never alone. God, the creator of the universe and all humankind, does not abandon his own. He is always with us, every step of the way, and on top of that he knows everything about us—every hair on our head (Luke 12:7), every desire of our heart (Ps. 139:13), every thought floating around in our brain. While we might be lonely at times, we are never alone.

It wasn't long before Christ brought me wonderful, holy, awesomely fun friends. These women loved the Lord, lived for the Lord, and, shockingly, were really normal. I felt like a fish out of water in the beginning because I had been one of those girls who had more guy friends than girlfriends and, consequently, didn't have a lot of practice in being a good girlfriend. I remember listening to one of my new friends, Christina, talk about what she was going to get her husband, Jay, for Christmas. She laughed about how she really wanted to get him some type of new kitchen gadget but wouldn't because it was too "self-fulfilling" and really a gift for her instead of him. This was news to me! Christina was actively trying to find a gift for her husband that he would love and that would serve him, not herself. Her words made me realize how often I served myself in my own life. I continue to learn from my girlfriends about how to be a more loving and beautiful daughter of God.

What are some other ways we can live out beautiful friendship? In all we do, we should ask ourselves, *How can I help my friend attain unity with God?* Like Laura and Kim, we can send our friends notes of encouragement, consolation, or advice. We can give our friends gifts that help them on their journey to heaven. We don't just have to give them books on prayer; we can give them things that help them fulfill their vocations in life. If you have a friend who is a mother, help her be a better mother. That might mean offering free babysitting so she can recharge, bringing her coffee one morning, or patiently listening to her concerns about one of her children. If you have a friend who is an accountant, encourage him to be the best accountant he can be. The basic lesson of being a friend is practicing empathy. What are the daily concerns and trials of your friends, and how can you walk with them as they journey toward Jesus?

After one of my husband's deployments, I asked him how he handles the moments of intense combat. I wondered if he had a rush of patriotism or maybe went into survival mode. If anyone met Ricky, you would never question his patriotism, respect, and loyalty to this country. However, his answer surprised me. Ricky told me, "Leah, you know I love our country and I joined the military to defend and protect it. But when I'm in the middle of a battle, I'm fighting for my teammates; I'm giving everything I got so that they can go home when this is all over."

Ricky's comment reflects Jesus' most beautiful offering to God the Father: himself on a cross so that we may go home. This is the type of friendship God offers us: his only Son who laid down his life for us. When we are willing to lay down our lives for our friends, we truly have beautiful friendships.

Beauty in Gratitude

We live in a consumerist culture, meaning we constantly buy things to find meaning in our lives. Americans buy $1.2

trillion worth of things they don't need every year.[16] We have trouble saying we have enough. We have trouble being grateful for the things we have. Beauty in gratitude, then, is a noticeable countercultural witness.

The people I think of first when I consider beauty in gratitude are my grandparents. My grandparents were very active in my life and, without a doubt, helped form me into the woman I am today. That's why it was incredibly difficult to watch my once-strong grandpa Dale battle cancer and be on the losing side. When he ended up in the hospital after years of battling multiple types of cancer and seemed to be nearing the end stages of life, my grandma Darlene never left his side.

My grandma has always been one of those people everyone notices. People often comment about her style and grace. Her style converges somewhere in the middle of three fashion icons: Grace Kelly, Audrey Hepburn, and Jackie Kennedy Onassis. I grew up with friends from grade school through graduate school who were in awe of her beauty. Sure, she has plenty of wrinkles and gray hair that made an appearance every once in a while between colorings, but there was something else about my grandma that radiated beauty. I saw it in her eyes, how she looked at you when you talked with her. I saw it in her hands when she held on to mine as we walked. She is special, there's no denying it.

But as she sat in the hospital, she was different. Grandma Darlene, who usually had her makeup applied perfectly, shed tears on a worn and grieving face. I could see the effect of her sorrow and weariness. Grandpa Dale had lost a significant amount of weight by that time and was literally skin and bones. All of the exterior beauty between the both of them seemed absent. That absence left an empty space to be filled with a beauty beyond what can be seen. When I think about it even now, those two were never more beautiful than in that time together in the hospital. If we look beyond the exterior standards of beauty, we can witness something honest and profound.

In what was to be one of their last conversations, my grandpa Dale sat up, held my grandma's hand, and said quietly, "Darlene, thank you for giving me such a great life." A short while later, he died, holding Grandma's hand and surrounded by family. While sorrowful, this moment between my grandparents was beautiful to witness because it displayed vulnerability and a deep sense of gratitude.

My grandparents' actions were beautiful. Two people embracing each other, one facing death and the other facing loss, yet still grateful for their life together. There is so much beauty in gratitude. Even in his last moments on earth, my grandpa lived and died beautifully. His gratitude, kindness, and love for my grandmother were a reflection of God. His life and death have inspired me to do the same, to live a beautiful life that is a reflection of truth and love and gratitude, which *is* beauty and *is* God.

We can exhibit beauty in gratitude in smaller ways too. We can take the time to write old-fashioned thank-you notes to those who give us gifts or do kind things for us, or we can take a moment to send an e-mail or text. We can generously tip our servers and say thank you sincerely with a smile rather than in a bored, routine way. We can choose to live a life of simplicity, asking of any given thing we want to buy, "Will this make my life more beautiful?" Each night before we go to sleep, we can list all the things that happened during the day that we are grateful for and give thanks to God for his blessings. You will be amazed how simply living a life of gratitude can help you grow in beauty.

Beauty in Speech

Another way we can exhibit beauty in action is through our speech. Jesus said, "But what comes out of the mouth proceeds from the heart" (Matt. 15:18). If true beauty starts inside of us, then our words, which proceed from the heart, need to reflect that beauty.

Research shows that girls say twice as many words a day as guys do.[17] So, especially for all of us ladies, learning how to speak eloquently, positively, and effectively is important. No one wants to be around someone who lacks tact, has a foul mouth, gossips uncontrollably, or never listens.

James chapter 3 has many challenging things to say about our words and how we use our tongues, such as "With it we bless the Lord and Father, and with it we curse men, who are made in the likeness of God. From the same mouth come blessing and cursing. My brethren, this ought not to be so" (vv. 9–10). As with any good thing, our mouths and our words can be used for good or for ill, as James points out. We want to use our words to glorify God and to affirm the good that others do.

In Holy Scripture Jesus warns us of the great power of words: "I tell you, on the day of judgment people will give account for every careless word they speak, for by your words you will be justified, and by your words you will be condemned" (Matt. 12:36–37 ESV). Our words should build up, speak truth, and in turn give glory to God: "Let no corrupting talk come out of your mouths, but only such as is good for building up, as fits the occasion, that it may give grace to those who hear" (Eph. 4:29 ESV).

One of the most common struggles we face with the use of words is gossip. Most people gossip because of insecurity, boredom, jealousy, revenge, to get attention, or to fit in, none of which stems from the kind of beauty we want to grow in our hearts. If you find yourself in a situation where this is happening, don't participate, but try to steer the conversation by either switching to another topic or saying something positive about the person being gossiped about. If all else fails, excuse yourself from the conversation.

Another newer form of speech that is far from beautiful is the sad reality of cyberbullying, the act of harassing someone online by posting mean, hurtful, and intimidating public or private messages or videos.

Researchers have found that positive words, both said and heard, increase cognitive reasoning, decrease stress, and can activate the motivational centers of the brain, propelling them into action. Meanwhile, negative words, both heard and said, can create havoc. When we allow negative words into our thoughts, they prevent certain neurochemicals that help with stress management from being released into the brain. This then increases the activity in the brain's fear center, the amygdala, and "partially shuts down the logic-and-reasoning centers located in the frontal lobes."[18] The negative words and stories that make up a cyberbullying attack not only defame the person they are directed at but negatively affect the bully as well.

Lizzie Velasquez knows the harmful effects of gossip and cyberbullying all too well. Velasquez has neonatal progeroid syndrome, a rare disease that affects her eyes, heart, and bones and prevents her from adding weight to her sixty-three-pound frame. In 2006 an anonymous person posted a video of Lizzie and titled it "The World's Ugliest Woman." The video went viral, and soon Lizzie accidentally found it online. The comments from the video were disgustingly hateful and even included tips on how she should kill herself. Lizzie's response to the video and the accompanying terrible comments was unexpected:

> Every time I thought I might be pretty, or that I'd finally fit in, or that maybe having this syndrome isn't so bad—all of that was demolished as soon as I found your post. I read through the thousands of comments under the video in desperation of finding just one comment that stood up for me. Did I find one? No . . . [T]he video you posted was the fuel to my fire. Your video took me to the lowest of lows, but over time, it made me stronger than I ever could have imagined. Your actions are what led me to learn how to pick myself back up again.[19]

Living out a beautiful life can sometimes get ugly, especially with how easy it is to use words in a less than godly way paired with today's world of anonymous online commentary. Lizzie could have easily sunk into depression and despair. She could have chosen not to fight back at all or to fight back with hate, but instead she chose to combat hate with beauty. In her documentary *A Brave Heart: The Lizzie Velasquez Story*, she says her life goal now is to spread kindness. "I knew this is my purpose, this is what I'm meant to do for the rest of my life because I like to think that I'm not only telling my story. I'm telling everyone's story."[20] Lizzie is now a motivational speaker and anti-bullying advocate, using her speech in a truly beautiful way. She has chosen to embrace her own God-given dignity and beauty to help others do the same.

Beauty in Generosity

In chapter 1 I pointed out that each year we as a society spend more on wearable fashion, cosmetics, and cosmetic surgeries than we do on donations to charitable causes. This is probably an effect of our individualistic culture that teaches us to think about ourselves first and others second. But the virtue of generosity flips that script. Beauty in generosity presents a countercultural witness that reflects the lavish generosity of God, who has given us every good thing.

We can be generous with the gifts God has bestowed upon us, such as money, but the truth about generosity is that a willing heart is all that is needed. You can be generous with your talents and gifts, but you can also be generous in other ways.

Listening to someone, noticing and acknowledging a person with a smile, or offering patience are just a few easy ways to incorporate the beauty of generosity into your daily life. Need is all around us. We all know someone who could use some help. Generosity guards against selfishness and greed. Be a blessing wherever you go, and you'll be blessed yourself.

Sean Forrest is one of those people who makes you shake your head and smile with admiration. He doesn't know how to be anything but generous with his life, resources, time, and love. Sean heard a call from God to help the people of Haiti, and since 2006 his organization Haiti180 has built a school, a home for the elderly, an orphanage, and a medical clinic. They offer mission trips throughout the year, hoping to cultivate a spirit and community of generosity. During one of these trips, Sean's friend, Dan, decided to go as well. Sean and Dan had gone to high school together and were even in the same rock-and-roll band at one point, but they had never had any in-depth talks about the meaning of life or God. So it was rather unexpected when Dan showed up in Haiti to help Sean with the mission.

Since Dan was in the country, Sean brought Dan to look at a plot of land the nonprofit was trying to purchase for the medical clinic. The Haitian man who owned the land, Mr. Joseph, came out to meet them. Mr. Joseph was barefoot, wearing rags that once were clothes; he lived in a shack across the street. After they greeted each other, Sean offered Mr. Joseph $8,000 for the land, but Mr. Joseph shook his head and said no.

Mr. Joseph explained, "You can't buy this land; it is a gift."

Sean, a little shocked, said, "What? No, this is too much. You need this money; this land could have provided crops for you and your family. If you won't take eight thousand dollars, then at least take four thousand."

Mr. Joseph interrupted Sean and said, "Stop. You're going to ruin my reward in heaven. God gave me this land, and now I need to give this land to the people of Haiti because a medical clinic here will save lives. If you give me money, you will ruin my reward in heaven." And with that, Mr. Joseph turned and walked back to his shack.

Sean started to walk after him but realized Dan was not with him anymore. Dan was back at the plot of land, just standing there. He had tears flowing down his face.

"What's wrong?" Sean asked.

Dan replied, "I've never seen such generosity in my entire life. I came here looking to find that kind of generosity, to see that kind of faith, because I've never seen it before, and now I have."

The generosity of Mr. Joseph not only provided the land for a medical clinic but renewed Dan's spirit. Truly, the beauty of generosity is that it reaches far beyond the dollar donated and touches the hearts of the people involved, leading them toward the God who gives us every good gift.

Beauty in Suffering

We all like to feel comfortable. Americans especially. We will do almost anything to avoid suffering or discomfort.

One concrete way we can see this in our culture is in how prescription drug use in the United States is at an all-time high. Three out of every five Americans take a prescription drug to avoid having to deal with pain. But let me assure you, at some point in your life, you will suffer.

One of your parents might get cancer. You might get cancer. Someone you know might be in a terrible auto accident. A friend might die unexpectedly. You might be unjustly fired from your job. Suffering is all around us in small and large ways. Our world does not know how to react to suffering. Often it leads to us questioning whether we're loved, whether God exists, and whether life has any meaning. So, like many Americans, we numb the pain. But suffering is actually our greatest opportunity to live a life of beauty. When it comes, will your life continue to point others back to Jesus?

Let's revisit what we previously named the most beautiful action in human history: the crucifixion of Jesus. Crucifixion was a terribly painful way to die. I won't go into all the gory details, but suffice it to say that the Romans were experts in pain. They wanted those who had been sentenced to death to experience the greatest pain for as long as possible, so they devised things like crucifixions that would not kill the victim immediately but would last for hours or days. In response to Jesus, God the Son, dying like a criminal on a cross, all of mankind has to pause and ask, "Why did he allow himself to suffer so much? He who performed miracles and raised men from the dead could have saved himself." He did it because he loved us to the end. His action was beautiful because it pointed to God's great love for all mankind. He died to unify us with the Father, to overcome the gulf that had been created by our sins.

Human suffering can have purpose when we choose to approach it in a beautiful way. We can complain, turn inward, hate God, and make sure everyone knows how miserable we are, or we can reflect on the suffering of God's only Son, unite our suffering with his, and use it as a catalyst to love others more deeply and draw them to God.

I was twelve years old when my grandpa was murdered. I grew up on a farm in Oklahoma, and my grandpa Darrow was one of our closest neighbors at a little less than five miles away. A few weeks after Christmas in 1991, Cooper James Scott, a hired hand on our farm, went over to my grandfather's house. He said he had a Christmas present to give my grandpa and kept fiddling with a brown grocery bag. After everyone gathered in the living room (my grandpa Darrow, his wife, their two kids, and a friend), Cooper pulled out a gun and ordered everyone to lie on the ground while he tied them up and gagged them. In the process of tying everyone up, Scott put down his gun. This is when my grandpa lunged for him in an attempt to protect and save his family. Scott pulled back quickly, grabbed his shotgun, and shot my grandfather. He died immediately of a gunshot wound to the head.

As soon as we heard the news, my parents gathered me and my siblings and went straight to church. We arrived at St. James Catholic Church in time for the 6:00 a.m. daily Mass. To say I was in shock was an understatement. This was the first time in my life that I had experienced evil. I knelt and began to get angry. Why would God allow this? I knew Cooper James Scott—he had helped out on our farm all the time—and I began feeling hate toward him. But as I looked up and fixed my eyes on the crucifix, I could feel God speak to my heart. I realized that God did indeed understand me and my feelings. His only begotten Son had been murdered too. I was not alone in my suffering.

Not only could God understand my suffering, but he could redeem and unite it with Christ's sufferings. As I reflected that morning on my suffering and Christ's suffering, I was convicted to forgive this man who had just killed my grandfather. I recalled the mercy Christ had given those who crucified him: "Father, forgive them, for they know not what they do" (Luke 23:34 ESV). I knew I had to begin the process of offering mercy to Scott. I could not allow hate to grow inside me. I needed to embrace the beauty of mercy, even and especially during times of intense suffering. Through this grace from God, my heart began to heal from great loss.

This is somewhat of an extreme example, but the truth is we can all live out beauty in suffering even in the smallest moments of life. When you're tired and there is a long checkout line at the store, instead of whining or being terse when you get to the clerk, ask them joyfully how their day was. When you stub your toe, instead of letting everyone know about it, unite it with Jesus' sufferings and joyfully continue on with your day. When someone gossips about you and causes you suffering by saying things that are not true, say something kind about them. Beauty manifested in joy can transform suffering and undo evils.

Living out a beautiful life might seem easy if we focus only on moments of comfort, but life itself is a haphazard, messy affair. A truly beautiful life is not a life void of trouble; instead, such a life embraces it all. Christ teaches us that even in suffering our lives can still be beautiful. And, yes, even our pain can be transformed if we unite it to the Lord, if we offer it to him who can redeem it, the One who suffers with us. Living out beauty in action, especially during times of suffering, reminds us that we are not alone in this life, even when it gets messy.

Living a Life of Beauty

A life of beauty is a life of wholeness and holiness. We can never forget our connection to God and to our neighbor and our duty to integrate beauty into every aspect of our lives. If we dare to call ourselves Christians, every detail of our lives should be a reflection of this truth. Through our dress, speech, and friendships; in our ability to show gratitude and generosity; and even in moments of intense suffering, we can put beauty on brilliant display. When we share our lives with others, even the messy parts, we cultivate a life of beauty that empowers us to embrace all circumstances. If we are willing to see with the eyes of God, we'll find beauty where we least expect it. In the words of Anne Frank, "Think of all the beauty still left around you and be happy."[21]

CONCLUSION

MY DAUGHTER, AGNES, WAS TWO YEARS OLD when we rushed her to the hospital via ambulance due to a severe asthma attack. Her breathing became so shallow that she lost consciousness. Thankfully, the doctors and nurses provided excellent care, and soon Agnes was on her way to recovery. During our stay in the NICU, Agnes received many pokes and prods from her nurses checking her IV, adjusting her meds, and so on, all of which were painful for her. I could tell Agnes was allowing fear to overwhelm and control her. Afraid that she was going to be hurt again, she would break down crying as soon as her nurses or doctor would enter the room. So I sat down with Agnes on her hospital bed and told her firmly, "Agnes, you are strong. You are brave. Do you understand me?" She nodded, and again I said to her, "Agnes, look at Mama. You *are* strong. You *are* brave."

Again, she nodded her head, and this time she sweetly said, "Okay, Mama. Okay."

I repeated this to her over and over every single day we

stayed in the hospital, and I made her repeat it back to me. Soon I witnessed a once fearful little girl become strong and brave. Agnes braved the nurses as they adjusted her IV or gave her shots. She believed me. She believed she was strong and brave.

A few months later, I gave birth to my third child, Violet, and brought her home to meet her big sister, Agnes, and big brother, Ambrose. Watching my three little gifts from God all gathered around me made for such a good day. Agnes and Ambrose were in awe at such a tiny little human, and the way they touched her displayed such care and gentleness.

After a few minutes, Agnes put her hand on Violet's head and stared at me with a curious look.

"What is it, Agnes?" I asked.

Agnes furrowed her brow, leaned in, and whispered, "Mom, is she strong and brave too?"

My heart about burst, and my eyes welled up with tears. I said, "Yes, Agnes. God made *all* girls strong and brave."

You, my sweet sisters, are strong and brave too. God made you that way. You are brave enough and strong enough to deny the world's limited definition of beauty and valiantly accept the beauty you've been made for and already have within you. The world's idea of beauty is shallow. It leads to brokenness, inwardness, and isolation. It's a type of rat race that can keep us running in circles until we are exhausted. Remember: "Even if you win the rat race, you're still a rat."[1]

The other side of beauty, the beauty that is God, never ends. It will always lead you to wholeness, holiness, and joy, because the way of beauty is the way of Christ Jesus.

This world needs beauty. *We* need real beauty. We need women who are brave enough to reclaim authentic beauty, to refuse the counterfeit and raise the bar so that all people will value each person over that person's parts. Invest in beauty. Invest in holiness. Rather than comparing and competing with others, look to the women of the world as companions, as your sisters in Christ. Offer a kind word, a compliment, or an encouragement for them in their search for beauty.

Here are some final tips to help you live out the beauty you are called to embrace and the beauty already within:

1. Appreciate how special you are.

    I've said it many times in this book, but I'm going to say it again: You've been made in the image and likeness of God! You haven't been made in the image and likeness of Chanel or MAC or any other substitute, but of your God who loves you and wants your happiness. You are unique and unrepeatable. No one else is just like you, and there will never be another you in this world. Your identity is found in God; you are a daughter of the King. Your worth is found in Christ, who conquered sin and death through his death and resurrection. And your beauty is found in the recognition and living out of your identity and worth. As Shannon Adler says, "You are not what others say you are. You are who God knows you are."[2]

2. Ditch comparison and embrace contribution.

    Can we just stop comparing ourselves with others?

If we believe God made us all unique and unrepeatable, then comparing ourselves to others makes zero sense. It's like a pineapple eyeing a mango and wishing it could have its smooth skin and unique flavor. Never gonna happen, and it shouldn't either. Don't compete. Don't compare. Instead, contribute. Contribute your friendship, gratitude, love, joy, and kindness to the world. W. L. Sheldon said, "There is nothing noble in being superior to your fellow men. True nobility lies in being superior to your former self."[3] Poet E. E. Cummings championed this same thought: "To be nobody-but-yourself—in a world which is doing its best, night and day, to make you everybody else—means to fight the hardest battle which any human being can fight; and never stop fighting."[4] Be who God made you to be, and be her well.

3. Forgive yourself.

There's beauty in finding peace within yourself. Everyone has to face their past mistakes at some point. Let it begin now, and forgive yourself. Maybe you dove deep into the world's idea of beauty and love and now are dealing with the consequences. Your life can get better. You do not have to live in regret. I am living proof of that. Pope John Paul II said, "We are not the sum of our weaknesses and failures; we are the sum of the Father's love for us."[5] Ask for God's forgiveness, and begin the healing process of forgiving yourself. Take courage, for Christ makes "all things new"

(Rev. 21:5). There will always be wounds that need healing in us and in the world, but remember, there is also more than enough love to heal them all.

4. Defend your beauty.

We've spent a good amount of time going over what authentic beauty is; now it's time to defend it. Take into account what triggers lead you into doubt, insecurity, vanity, and anything else that goes against true beauty. It might be what you watch on television, what you read, which friends you hang out with, the time spent on social media or apps, or even the groups or people you follow online. If any of these make you feel that you are less than a daughter of God or do not breathe joy and peace into your life, let it go. Proverbs 4:23 tells us the importance of protecting our innermost self: "Above all else, guard your heart, for everything you do flows from it" (NIV). Imitation beauty will always make you feel like you are not enough. You are enough, and you're worth defending. Your beauty is beyond what you or others can see. The beauty of who you are is whose you are.

5. Let Love love you.

"'The LORD your God is in your midst, a mighty one who will save; he will rejoice over you with gladness; he will quiet you by his love'" (Zeph. 3:17 ESV). In the end it all comes down to this: Father, child, love. God is the Father, we are his children, and he loves us. Let him. Let God, who is beauty, love you.

Everything depends on your relationship with Christ. I encourage you to accept him into your life; let him transform you, heal you, and make you new. Christ died for you, but remember, he also rose for you. Let the powerful risen Christ love you, and then let this love inspire the world.

6. Do something beautiful.

   True beauty unites, affirms worth, and loves. True beauty is humble and honest, yet powerful. Beauty in action is the force that will help send truth and love out into the world. Albert Einstein said, "The ideals that have lighted my way, and time after time have given me new courage to face life cheerfully, have been Kindness, Beauty, and Truth."[6] How will you use the beauty of your life to effect positive change? You do not need an advanced degree, money, or status to do something beautiful. All you need is you. You have the duty and power to fill the world with the light of goodness, beauty, and truth through your words and actions. Never underestimate the power of a kind smile, a generous word, or a loving touch. These are all ways we can do something beautiful and in turn make this world a little brighter.

   In fact, there are people waiting for your light. The lonely, the forgotten, the suffering—they're all waiting for someone to show them beauty, to remind them of their dignity and worth. And you have the power to reflect this to the world. You have the power to bring the beauty of your life to another. You may be the only copy of the gospel people will ever read. Live out the beauty of the gospel of Jesus Christ, and share that beauty with others. "If you are what you should be, you will set the whole world ablaze!"[7]

———

I pray this book has given you something to ponder when it comes to your beauty inside and out. I pray this book has encouraged all of us women to proudly wear our faith, whether that is with a little black dress, jeans, or a uniform.

> The hour is coming, in fact has come, when the vocation of women is being acknowledged in its fullness, the hour in which women acquire in the world an influence, an effect and a power never hitherto achieved. That is why, at this moment when the human race is undergoing so deep a transformation, women imbued with a spirit of the Gospel can do so much to aid humanity in not falling.[8]

Let us create an influence, an effect, and a power in the world that uplifts women's dignity, embraces our differences, and aims to bring the love and beauty of Christ to others.

The world needs you. Beauty needs you. Now go, and do something beautiful for God.

And when night comes, and you look back over the day and see how fragmentary everything has been, and how much you planned that has gone undone, and all the reasons you have to be embarrassed and ashamed: just take everything exactly as it is, put it in God's hands and leave it with Him. Then you will be able to rest in Him—really rest—and start the next day as a new life.

—Edith Stein

APPENDIX A

THE NEVER LIST

by Beautycounter™

Benzalkonium chloride: a disinfectant used as a preservative and surfactant associated with severe skin, eye, and respiratory irritation and allergies. Found in: sunscreens, moisturizers.

BHA and BHT: synthetic antioxidants used to extend shelf life. They are likely carcinogens and hormone disruptors and may cause liver damage. Found in: lipsticks, moisturizers, diaper creams, and other cosmetics.

Coal-tar hair dyes and other coal-tar ingredients: a by-product of coal processing that is a known carcinogen. It is used as a colorant and an anti-dandruff agent. Found in: hair dye, shampoo.

Ethylenediaminetetraacetic acid (EDTA): a chelating (binding) agent added to cosmetics to improve stability. May be toxic to organs. Found in: hair color, moisturizers.

Ethanolamines (MEA/DEA/TEA): surfactants and pH adjuster linked to allergies, skin toxicity, hormone disruption, and inhibited fetal brain development. Found in: hair dyes, mascara, foundation, fragrances, sunscreens, dry-cleaning solvents, paint, pharmaceuticals.

Formaldehyde: used as a preservative in cosmetics. A known carcinogen that is also linked to asthma, neurotoxicity, and developmental toxicity. Present where quaternium-15, DMDM hydantoin, imidazolidinyl urea, diazolidinyl urea, sodium hydroxymethylglycinate, 2-bromo-2-nitropropane-1,3 diol (Bronopol), and several other preservatives are listed. Found in: shampoo, body wash, bubble bath.

Hydroquinone: a skin-lightening chemical that inhibits the production of melanin and is linked to cancer, organ toxicity, and skin irritation. Found in: skin-lightening creams.

Methylisothiazolinone and methylchloroisothiazolinone: chemical preservatives that are among the most common irritants, sensitizers, and causes of contact skin allergies. Found in: shampoo, conditioner, body wash.

Oxybenzone: sunscreen agent and ultraviolet-light absorber linked to irritation, sensitization, and allergies, and possible hormone disruption. Found in: sunscreen, moisturizer.

Parabens (methyl-, isobutyl-, propyl-, and others): a class of preservatives commonly used to prevent the growth of bacteria and mold. Parabens are endocrine (or hormone) disruptors, which may alter important hormone mechanisms in our bodies. Found in: shampoo, face cleanser, body wash, body lotion, foundation.

Phthalates (DBP, DEHP, DEP, and others): a class of plasticizing chemicals used to make products more pliable or to make fragrances stick to skin. Phthalates disrupt the endocrine system and may cause birth defects. Found in: synthetic fragrance, nail polish, hairspray, and plastic materials.

Polyethylene glycol (PEG compounds): PEGs are widely used in cosmetics as thickeners, solvents, softeners, and moisture carriers. Depending on manufacturing processes, PEGs may be contaminated with measurable amounts of ethylene oxide and 1,4-dioxane, which are both carcinogens. Found in: creams, sunscreen, shampoo.

Sodium lauryl sulfate and sodium laureth sulfate (SLS and SLES): SLS and SLES are surfactants that can cause skin irritation or trigger allergies. SLES is often contaminated with 1,4-dioxane, a byproduct of a petrochemical process called ethoxylation, which is used to process other chemicals in order to make them less harsh. Found in: shampoo, body wash, bubble bath.

Synthetic flavor or fragrance: an engineered scent or flavoring agent that may contain any combination of three thousand or more stock chemical ingredients, including hormone disruptors and allergens. Fragrance formulas are protected under federal law's classification of trade secrets and therefore can remain undisclosed. Found in: all types of cosmetics.

Toluene: a volatile petrochemical solvent that is toxic to the immune system and can cause birth defects. Found in: nail polish.

Triclosan and triclocarban: antimicrobial pesticides toxic to the aquatic environment; may also impact human reproductive systems. Found in: liquid soap, soap bars, toothpaste.

APPENDIX B

LEAH'S MODESTY GUIDELINES

Your dresses should be tight enough to show you're
a woman and loose enough to show you're a lady.

—EDITH HEAD

As I mentioned before, these general guidelines are ones I use and have found helpful in showing respect to myself. These common sense modest fashion guidelines help celebrate our dignity (and style) yet do not reduce us to a collection of body parts. Of course, reasonable people can disagree on specifics, especially regarding dignified dress for certain places and occasions. So if your parents, places of worship, or other communities require more than my guidelines suggest, I encourage you to follow their guidelines for that particular place or occasion. Your wardrobe should always show respect to the people and organizations you value.

How can you tell if clothing is too tight? It's too tight when:

- Undergarment lines or details can be seen through the fabric.
- Skin is bulging out of undergarments.
- You have to pull up your jeans like leggings or lie on the bed to get them on.
- Shirts buckle when buttoned up.
- Fabrics, when zipped, bunch up (they should lie flat across the skin).
- You're unable to hug someone because your arms are restrained.
- Your pants create a muffin top. (There is actually a medical condition for this called *tight pants syndrome*, with symptoms including abdominal pain, heartburn, and reflux.)
- Your pencil skirt shows horizontal lines when sitting or rides up when walking.
- Horizontal ridges appear right below your backside when wearing jeans/pants.
- You cannot pull any material away from the center of your thigh.

Women should be two things: classy and fabulous.

—Coco Chanel

How can you tell if it's too short?

- Dresses and skirts will get shorter when you sit. Before heading out the door, see what it looks like sitting down or crossing your legs.

- If your skirt or dress hits above the knee, high heels will automatically make it appear shorter. A general rule is the higher the heel, the longer the dress/skirt should be.
- Choose shorts/dresses/skirts whose lower hems extend past your arms. Hold your arms straight down at your sides. Keep your fingers extended, and make sure that the lower hem falls below the longest finger.

Modesty is the highest elegance.

—Coco Chanel

How low is too low?

- Purposely displaying cleavage, or what I like to call cupeths-that-overfloweth, is never classy. Your top should at least cover your chest so no cleavage is showing. Yes, we all know you're a woman. We all have boobs. Now, let's keep 'em covered and move on.
- Generally, there is nothing wrong with showing your shoulders. However, please be respectful of different rules that may apply at a church, temple, or synagogue. A wrap, scarf, or cardigan is always a good item to have on hand.
- Strapless tops can be tricky. The problem with most strapless tops is not that they expose your shoulders, but that you are not fully supported. The purpose of straps is to hold the top up. If you're constantly adjusting or pulling up your top, you need those straps.
- Straps that are at least a couple of inches thick still

allow for undergarments to be worn with ease. Yes, I know strapless bras exist, but they lack comfort and proper support. Your fashions should not require your attention every time you move!

> Beauty without modesty is like a
> conversation without honesty.
>
> —Boonaa Mohammed

Fashion No-Nos:

- Wearing leggings as pants. Leggings aren't pants. If they were, they'd be called pants, but they're not. They're leggings. If you wear them, make sure your top covers your backside.
- Undergarments on display. Undergarments should not be outer garments or show through clothing.
- Clothes that need constant adjustment (they're not worth your time; give them up!).
- Words plastered onto your chest or butt. Your body is not a billboard. Steer clear of fashion that makes your body parts a brand's personal marketing committee.

> Modesty is always beautiful.
>
> —G. K. Chesterton

Tips and Quick Fixes:

- Camisoles are the perfect quick fix to plunging necklines or tops that are either too low or gape open at the top.

- Short skirts or dresses can be paired with leggings or tights in a fun color.
- Many skirts and dresses have around one to two inches of extra fabric that you can let out if you require more material.
- If you have trouble getting into or out of an outfit, let it go or go up a size.
- If, when you look in the mirror, your eyes are drawn to one of your body parts first and not your face, it's possible this is the area that needs adjustment.

APPENDIX C

THE CLOSET CHALLENGE:

Seven Items for Thirty Days

The goal of the Closet Challenge is to simplify our lives. Jesus helped me learn more about myself through this simplification process, and he will help you too. He stripped me of the idea that my clothes or what people think of me make me who I am. I am more than this; you are more than this. God has called us by name; he anticipates us, and he has a plan for us. I encourage you to let him into your life—even into your wardrobe.

> "Is not life more than food, and the body more than clothing? . . . And why are you anxious about clothing? Consider the lilies of the field, how they grow; they neither toil nor spin; yet I tell you, even Solomon in all his glory was not arrayed like one of these. But if God so clothes the grass of the field, which today is alive and

tomorrow is thrown into the oven, will he not much more clothe you, O men of little faith?" (Matt. 6:25, 28–30)

How-To: The Closet Challenge

- Pick out seven separate items of clothing.
- Hang your seven items outside of your closet to help limit distractions or temptations.
- Share with your friends this journey you're about to take, and invite them along.
- Take pictures of yourself in your Closet Challenge outfits along the way. You might be surprised how many people will be inspired to take up the challenge once they see someone actually doing it.
- Use the hashtag #TheClosetChallenge on social media to document your journey.

Now, we are not savages. We've built a fair number of freebies into this challenge so you don't get too stinky or freaked out about wearing skinny jeans to the gym.

Freebies

- Undergarments
- Tank tops/camis (to use as undershirts for coverage/modesty)

- Shoes
- Accessories (jewelry, scarves)
- Outerwear, such as coats
- Bathing suits
- Pajamas
- Gym clothes (worn at the gym, not to be a daily outfit)

The Aftermath

I have completed this challenge multiple times and have learned a few things that I hope will inspire you to take up the challenge yourself.

1. Less is more

Having fewer options to choose from has made my life a whole lot easier. You know that feeling you get when you're staring at your closet stuffed full of clothing and think you have nothing to wear, or that nothing fits, or that nothing is in style? That feeling never happened once for me during the thirty days of the challenge. Setting aside a few pieces that I *know* look good on me and fit me made it easier to get dressed quickly and move on with my day.

We have this idea that more is better. But more is just more. Having more options doesn't guarantee we'll be happier. If that was the case, every time I walked into Sephora I'd feel amazing. Instead, I feel overwhelmed and have no idea where to start to get the best red lipstick (still searching).

2. I'm not the center of attention

To be honest, I feared people would notice if I wore the same few outfits all the time. But other than those who took on the challenge with me, no one noticed. Why? Because I'm not the center of the universe. And that actually feels good. The beauty of simplicity is that it is others-centered, not self-centered.

3. More time for what really matters

The Closet Challenge helped me eliminate my daily wardrobe-therapy session (freaking out about what still doesn't fit me since having a baby or not feeling in-style enough for the cool kids on the block), which in turn allowed me to have more time for what really matters, like my husband and my kids. I even had more time to give others when I was traveling and speaking. Why? Because I wasn't wasting any time on choosing what to wear. I knew my choices, threw on an outfit, and got on with my life. I'm shocked at how much time I have wasted getting dressed in the mornings, choosing what to pack in my suitcase, and trying on multiple outfits in hotel rooms on the road just so I could attain a certain look. Making time for what really matters is what really matters.

ACKNOWLEDGMENTS

WHAT A WONDERFUL PROBLEM TO HAVE WHEN there are so many people to express gratitude toward. This book you hold in your hands could not have been dreamt, written, or published without the souls mentioned below, and many more I hold near and dear to my heart.

Ricky, I'll never forget the gift God gave me as the church doors opened and I saw you at the end of the aisle. Peace, God's peace, filled my soul as I looked at you. You've always been the one for me. From our first date, to just being friends, to dating again, and then to that evening on June 29 when we changed eternity by marrying each other. Thank you, Ricky, for being my solid number two and never allowing Christ to slip from that number one spot in my life. Thank you for never giving up on me, on us, on the work God is doing in me and in the world. Thank you for loving me at my lowest, for seeing the ugly and broken in me and still embracing me with the sweetest of loves. If today was June 29, 2012, I'd still choose you. And always will. *Totus Tuus!*

Agnes, Ambrose, and Violet, you are my sweet little

jewels. I love you more than the stars in the sky, more than all the flowers and even more than the unicorns at the end of every rainbow (according to Agnes). You bring me the sweetest joy and remind me exactly what true beauty is. It is you: innocent, exploring souls who find joy in muddy puddles, ice cream with sprinkles, dancing to made-up songs, and backyard picnics. You are a gift, your life is a gift—make sure you share it with others.

Mom, you are the true underdog, and as a new mother myself, I realize this is the fate of all mothers. We toil day and night, praying for our children, guiding them, cleaning up after them, cooking meals, providing clean clothes, and making sure they survive another day. All this and I still put you through so much grief for ten years. I'm sorry, Mom. I'm sorry I took for granted your love, your faith in me, and your faith in the power of the Holy Spirit. Thank you for always being there, and always leaving the door open for God. You taught me how to be honest with myself, to accept my limitations but to never put any on God. I pray I can become a mother like you.

Dad. Well, Dad, you've been there for everything. You and Mom brought me into this world, and with God's grace, you were the one who helped me leave living for the world. You see me for who I really am: broken and redeemed. And yet, you still love me and still sport that big, silly grin that I saw the same day you came to pick me up from New York. Thank you for working so hard, every day, for all of us. Every choice made, every penny spent was done for the betterment of our family. What a gift you are to this world and us! You are the quiet saint, the unsung hero, but more than all that, you are *my* Dad. And I love you!

My brothers and sisters, Angela, Daniel, Matthew, David, and Elizabeth. Thank you for loving me and accepting me when I've been "the worst." Thank you for helping me put all the pieces back together, for your prayers, and for all the ridiculous ways you make me laugh, even if they are slightly inappropriate. You are my best friends.

Alicia Bungum, I think you and I both know this work would never have seen the light of day if it wasn't for your ability to make clear what were just muddy ideas in my head. Thank you for always asking me the question of, "What's the point?" for every single word written. You made me dig deep with this work to uncover the gems my heart was waiting to share with the world, as well as adding profound theological insights to what my heart was trying to get at. You were able to translate my heart at times when I was unable to do so. Thank you, my friend. Thanks also to your husband Donnie and your three sweet babies for sharing you with me and this work.

Grandpa Dale, you were the first person to ever suggest I should write a book. Little did I know, over twenty years later, here I am and here's the book. When I asked you what I should write about, you told me, "write what you know." This is it. What I know is that God still loves me broken, heals me, and makes me new in Him. I now know that Jesus is the other side of beauty—the beauty that transforms and saves. I love you, Grandpa, and I miss you every day. But I am at peace knowing you are in the presence of the Beautiful One.

My Squad: Sarah Swafford, Sarah Kroger, Jackie Angel, Emily Wilson, Sr. Miriam, Lisa Cotter, Natalie Stefanick, Molly Vernon, and Liz Mallory. Every single one of you has added so much beauty to my life. You've made me better. You've allowed me to be vulnerable with you, to share my heart, worries, joys, and more importantly—my life. You are life-giving friends. And those are the best kinds of friends. I love you, and thank you, for making me more beautiful through your friendship.

Thank you to Erik Wolgemuth, my literary agent. Thank you for championing this cause with me years ago, letting me dream for as long as I needed, and for the encouragement to press on during those long days of writing.

A very, very special thanks goes to my phenomenal Thomas Nelson team and publisher. Thank you for taking a chance on me, for your belief that more women need to be reminded of their beauty within, and for giving my heart a voice in the written world. I am so grateful to work with you and to be a part of the Thomas Nelson family.

ABOUT THE AUTHOR

LEAH DARROW IS AN INTERNATIONAL SPEAKER, writer, wife to a US Army Green Beret, and mom to three marvelous, crazy little kids. As a former model and contestant on *America's Next Top Model*, Leah has a driving passion to explore fashion's ability to empower women and highlight their irreplaceable worth. Besides kayaking with orcas with her hubby, nothing is more exciting to her than helping women discover their true beauty and goodness in Christ.

Leah earned a bachelor's degree in psychology from the University of Missouri–St. Louis and a master's degree in theology from the Augustine Institute. Besides leading Bible studies, grabbing coffee with girlfriends, or washing the newest mystery stain out of her clothes, Leah can frequently be found at Busch Stadium cheering on the St. Louis Cardinals, enjoying a glass of wine on her front-porch swing, or unabashedly singing and dancing with her children in the front yard.

NOTES

Chapter 1: The World's Definition of Beauty

1. Badger & Winters, The Girls Lounge, and Advertising Benchmark Index, "Quantifying the Effect of Objectifying Women in Advertising," Women Not Objects, accessed December 3, 2016, http://womennotobjects.com/s/BW _Objectifying-Women-in-Advertising.pdf.

2. "About Maybelline," Maybelline.com, accessed May 8, 2017, https://www.maybelline.com/about-maybelline.

3. United States Congress Joint Economic Committee, "The Economic Impact of the Fashion Industry," September 2016, https://www.jec.senate.gov/public/?a=Files.Serve&File _id=66DBA6DF-E3BD-42B4-A795-436D194EF08A.

4. American Society for Aesthetic Plastic Surgery, "American Society for Aesthetic Plastic Surgery Reports More Than $13.5 Billion Spent for the First Time Ever," Surgery.org, March 8, 2016, http://www.surgery.org/media/news-releases/american -society-for-aesthetic-plastic-surgery-reports-more-than-135 -billion-spent-for-the-first-time-ever.

5. "SEAT Unveils the Mii by Cosmopolitan," SEAT, September 16, 2016, http://www.seat.co.uk/about-seat/news-events/events /seat-unveils-new-mii-by-cosmopolitan.html.

6. "The Seat Mii by Cosmopolitan Is Finally Here," *Cosmopolitan*,

September 16, 2016, http://www.cosmopolitan.com/uk
/entertainment/a45920/seamii-cosmopolitan-car-launch/.

7. Brielle Saggese, "The History of Shaving: Why Do We Hate
Our Body Hair?" The Lala, May 1, 2016, http://thelala.com
/women-start-shaving-history-hate-body-hair/.

8. Lulu Garcia-Navarro, "In Brazil, Nips and Tucks Don't Raise an
Eyebrow," NPR, October 7, 2014, http://www.npr.org/sections
/parallels/2014/10/07/353270270/an-uplifting-story-brazils
-obsession-with-plastic-surgery.

9. Ellen DeGeneres, "Bic Pens for Women," video, 4:08, Ellentv
.com, October 12, 2012, http://www.ellentv.com/2012/10/12
/bic-pens-for-women/.

10. Anna Bessendorf, "From Cradle to Cane: The Cost of Being
a Female Consumer, A Study of Gender Pricing in New York
City," New York City Department of Consumer Affairs,
December 2015, 11, https://www1.nyc.gov/assets/dca/downloads
/pdf/partners/Study-of-Gender-Pricing-in-NYC.pdf.

11. Ibid., 28.

12. Ibid., 21.

13. Ibid., 5.

14. Jean O'Brien, "Giving USA: 2015 Was America's Most-Generous
Year Ever," Giving USA, June 13, 2016, https://givingusa.org
/giving-usa-2016/.

15. *Chasing Beauty*, directed by Brent Huff, performed by Kelly
Anderson, Jo Baker, William Barney (USA: Logo Television
Network, 2013), documentary film.

Chapter 2: The Hight Cost of Imitation Beauty

1. "Cohabiter Vows," YouTube video, 1:43, posted by Charles
Pope, April 13, 2011, https://www.youtube.com/watch?v
=XVErKZGzNNM.

2. Scott M. Stanley, Galena K. Rhoades, and Sarah W. Whitton,
"Commitment: Functions, Formation, and the Securing of

Romantic Attachment," *Journal of Family Theory & Review* 2, no. 4 (December 2010): 243–57.

3. "Pope Francis Denounces Abortion after Decrying Church's Focus on Rules," CBS News, September 20, 2013, http://www .cbsnews.com/news/pope-francis-denounces-abortion-after -decrying-churchs-focus-on-rules/.

4. Bill Chameides, "Lipstick: The Price for Pretty Lips May Be Heavy . . . Metals," *Huffington Post*, May 9, 2013, www .huffingtonpost.com/bill-chameides/lipstick-the-price-for-pr_b _3248095.html.

5. The Campaign for Safe Cosmetics, "International Laws," SafeCosmetics.org, accessed May 15, 2017, http://www .safecosmetics.org/get-the-facts/regulations/international-laws/.

6. "The Personal Care Products Safety Act: Modernizing Outdated Regulations," Society for Women's Health Research, January 5, 2016, https://lawstreetmedia.com/issues/health-science/the-personal -care-products-safety-act-modernizing-outdated-regulations/).

7. University of North Carolina at Chapel Hill School of Medicine, "Survey Finds Disordered Eating Behaviors among Three out of Four American Women," UNC.edu, April 22, 2008, http:// www.med.unc.edu/www/newsarchive/2008/april/survey-finds -disordered-eating-behaviors-among-three-out-of-four-american -women.

8. "Women and Tobacco Use," American Lung Association, http:// www.lung.org/stop-smoking/smoking-facts/women-and-tobacco -use.html.

9. Ibid.

10. Mario Palmer, "5 Facts about Body Image," Amplify, accessed February 24, 2014, webpage no longer available.

11. "'Cleansing' Diets May Be Worthless, Dangerous," Fox News, September 20, 2006, http://www.foxnews.com/story/2006 /09/20/cleansing-diets-may-be-worthless-dangerous.html.

12. Ibid.

13. American Psychological Association, "Developing Adolescents:

A Reference for Professionals," 2002, 16, 31, http://www.apa
.org/pi/families/resources/develop.pdf.

14. M. E. Collins, "Body Figure Perceptions and Preferences
among Pre-Adolescent Children," *International Journal of Eating
Disorders* 10, no. 2 (1991), 199–208, https://www.national
eatingdisorders.org/get-facts-eating-disorders.

15. L. Mellin, S. McNutt, Y. Hu, G. B. Schreiber, P. Crawford, and
E. Obarzanek, "A Longitudinal Study of the Dietary Practices
of Black and White Girls 9 and 10 Years Old at Enrollment:
The NHLBI Growth and Health Study," *Journal of Adolescent
Health* 20, no. 1 (1997), 27–37, https://www.nationaleating
disorders.org/get-facts-eating-disorders.

16. Alison E. Field et. al, "Exposure to the Mass Media and Weight
Concerns among Girls," *Pediatrics* 103, no. 3 (March 1999), 1,
http://pediatrics.aappublications.org/content/103/3/e36.

17. Name has been changed.

18. Jennifer L. Greenberg et.al, "How Is BDD Treated?"
International OCD Foundation, accessed May 2, 2017, https://
bdd.iocdf.org/about-bdd/how-is-bdd-treated/#cbt.

19. Dove Self-Esteem Project, "Women in the Media: Is It Time
to Give the Media Stereotypes a Makeover?" June 26, 2013,
accessed January 18, 2017, http://selfesteem.dove.us/Articles
/Written/Women_in_media_is_it_time_to_give_the_media
_stereotypes_a_makeover.aspx.

20. Ibid.

21. Ibid.

22. *The True Cost*, directed by Andrew Morgan (Sherman Oaks,
CA: Untold Creative, 2015), documentary film, https://
truecostmovie.com.

23. Jim Yardley, "Report on Deadly Factory Collapse in Bangladesh
Finds Widespread Blame," *New York Times*, May 22, 2013,
http://www.nytimes.com/2013/05/23/world/asia/report-on
-bangladesh-building-collapse-finds-widespread-blame.html.

24. Ibid.

Chapter 3: False Love and the Pursuit of Worth

1. Thomas Aquinas, *Summa Theologiae* I.20.1, reply to ob. 3.
2. J. Spencer, G. Zimet, M. Aalsma, and D. Orr, "Self-Esteem as a Predictor of Initiation of Coitus in Early Adolescents," *Pediatrics* 109, no. 4 (April 2002), 581–84.
3. Augustine, *Confessions* 4.13.20.
4. Quentyn Kennemer, "Android Has 1 Billion Active Users in the Past 30 Days (And Other Interesting Numbers from IO)," Phandroid, June 25, 2014, http://phandroid.com/2014/06/25 /android-has-1-billion-active-users-in-the-past-30-days-and -other-interesting-numbers-from-io/.

Chapter 4: The Truth About Beauty

1. Philip Kosloski, "6 Inspiring Stories from People Who Met Mother Teresa," Aleteia.org, September 2, 2016, http://aleteia.org /2016/09/02/6-inspiring-stories-from-people-who-met-mother -teresa/.
2. Aquinas, *Summa Theologiae* I–II.27.1, reply to ob. 3.
3. Ibid., I.39.8.
4. Charles Feng, "Looking Good: The Psychology and Biology of Beauty," *Journal of Young Investigators* 6, no. 6 (December 2002), http://legacy.jyi.org/volumes/volume6/issue6/features/feng.html.
5. Ibid.
6. Fulton Sheen, Twitter post, August 23, 2012, 7:13 a.m., https:// twitter.com/fultonsheen/status/238640168343584769.
7. Thomas Dubay. *The Evidential Power of Beauty* (San Francisco: Ignatius, 1999), 41.
8. Benedict XVI, "The *Via Pulchritudinis*: Privileged Pathway for Evangelisation and Dialogue" (concluding document of the plenary assembly of the Pontifical Council for Culture, March 27–28, 2006), III.3, http://www.vatican.va/roman_curia /pontifical_councils/cultr/documents/rc_pc_cultr_doc_20060327 _plenary-assembly_final-document_en.html#_Toc135891125

9. Irenaeus, *Against Heresies*, 4.20.7. http://www.touchstonemag
   .com/archives/article.php?id=25–05-003-e#ixzz4imE34P9h.

Chapter 5: Desiring Beauty

1. Aaron Smith, "Part IV: Cell Phone Attachment and Etiquette,"
   Pew Research Center, November 30, 2012, http://www.pew
   internet.org/2012/11/30/part-iv-cell-phone-attachment
   -and-etiquette/.
2. Ibid.
3. Jean Arp, *Arp on Arp: Poems, Essays, Memories* (New York: Viking,
   1972), 231.
4. C. S. Lewis, "Letter XXII" in *The Screwtape Letters* (Grand Rapids:
   Zondervan, 2007), 249.
5. Spiritual Knowledge and Discrimination, 85
6. Scott Hahn, Curtis Mitch, and Dennis Walters, "Commentary
   on John 4:38," in *Ignatius Catholic Study Bible: Revised Standard
   Version*, 2nd ed. (San Francisco: Ignatius, 1999), 169.
7. Francis I, *"Evangelii Gaudium"* (apostolic exhortation, St. Peter's
   Basilica, Rome, Italy, November 24, 2013), I.3, http://w2.vatican
   .va/content/francesco/en/apost_exhortations/documents/papa
   -francesco_esortazione-ap_20131124_evangelii-gaudium.html
   #I.%E2%80%82A_joy_ever_new,_a_joy_which_is_shared.
8. John Paul II, "Christian Response to Modern Atheism" (general
   audience, April 14, 1999), https://w2.vatican.va/content/john-paul
   -ii/en/audiences/1999/documents/hf_jp-ii_aud_14041999.html.

Chapter 6: Becoming Beautiful

1. *Catechism of the Catholic Church* (Liguori, MO: Liguori
   Publications, 1994), article 2520.
2. Catholic Answers, "What Is Chastity?" Chastity.com, accessed
   January 19, 2017, http://chastity.com/what-is-chastity.
3. *Catechism of the Catholic Church*, article 2339.
4. Paul VI, "Lumen Gentium" (Second Vatican Council, St. Peter's

Basilica, Rome, Italy, November 21, 1964), article 40, http://
www.vatican.va/archive/hist_councils/ii_vatican_council
/documents/vat-ii_const_19641121_lumen-gentium_en.html.

5. "Spanish Model Quits Glamorous Career to Become a Nun,"
June 23, 2014, Catholic.org, http://www.catholic.org/news/hf
/faith/story.php?id=55906.

6. Catholic News Agency, "Former Colombian Model Shares
Conversion Story," May 25, 2010, CatholicNewsAgency.com,
http://www.catholicnewsagency.com/news/former-colombian
-model-shares-conversion-story/.

7. Kylie Bisutti, Twitter post, December 21, 2011, https://twitter
.com/mrsbisutti/status/149589046451122177; Post Staff Report,
"I Gave Up Modeling for God," New York Post, April 24, 2013,
http://nypost.com/2013/04/24/i-gave-up-modeling-for-god/.

8. Nicole Weider, "About Nicole," Project Inspired, accessed
May 4, 2017, http://www.projectinspired.com/about-nicole/.

9. John Paul II, *The Meaning of Vocation* (Princeton, NJ: Scepter
Publishers, 1997), 21.

10. Ibid., 13.

Chapter 7: Sharing Beauty

1. Benedict XVI, "Meeting with Artists in the Sistine Chapel"
(speech, the Sistine Chapel, Vatican City, November 21, 2009),
https://w2.vatican.va/content/benedict-xvi/en/speeches/2009
/november/documents/hf_ben-xvi_spe_20091121_artisti.html.

2. Fulton Sheen, *Life Is Worth Living* (San Francisco: Ignatius Press,
1999), 255.

3. *Catechism of the Catholic Church,* article 2524.

4. Ibid., article 2521.

5. Ibid.

6. Siofra Brennan, "The Duchess of Demure: Kate Adds Modesty
Panels to Make Her £795 Green Lace Temperley Dress Less
Racy for a Meeting with the Indian Prime Minister in Delhi,"

Daily Mail Online, April 13, 2016, http://www.dailymail.co.uk /femail/article-3535429/Kate-adds-modesty-panels-795-Temperley -dress-India-visit.html.

7. Piercarlo Valdesolo, "How Our Brains Turn Women into Objects," *Scientific American*, October 11, 2011, https://www .scientificamerican.com/article/how-our-brains-turn-women -into-objects/.

8. LiveScience Staff, "Men and Women Literally See the World Differently," Mother Nature Network, September 4, 2012, https:// www.mnn.com/health/fitness-well-being/stories/men-and-women -literally-see-the-world-differently; Robin Nixon, "Matters of the Brain: Why Men and Women Are So Different," Live Science, May 1, 2012, http://www.livescience.com/20011-brain-cognition -gender-differences.html.

9. M. Tiggemann and R. Andrew, "Clothes Make a Difference: The Role of Self-Objectification," *Sex Roles* 66, no. 9/10 (2012), 646.

10. Ibid.

11. APA Task Force, *Report of the APA Task Force on the Sexualization of Girls* (Washington, DC: American Psychological Association, 2007), 4, http://www.apa.org/pi/women/programs/girls/report.aspx.

12. Ibid, 8.

13. These guidelines are not an exhaustive list, but a quick guide to modest dressing. Different cultures, customs and religions may require additional or varying guidelines.

14. Fashion guidelines taken from *Decent Exposure*, which I wrote with Jessica Rey. Find out more at http://www.decentexposure online.com/.

15. Donna-Marie Cooper O'Boyle, "Mother Teresa and Me: Ten Years of Friendship" (Huntington, IN: Our Sunday Visitor, 2009), 116.

16. Mark Whitehouse, "Number of the Week: Americans Buy More Stuff They Don't Need," *Real Time Economics* (blog), *Wall Street Journal*, April 23, 2011, http://blogs.wsj.com/economics/2011/04/23 /number-of-the-week-americans-buy-more-stuff-they-dont-need/.

17. Eliza Collins, "Who Talks More: Men or Women?" *USA Today*,

February 21, 2013, https://www.usatoday.com/story/news/nation
/2013/02/21/girls-talk-more/1935963/#.

18. Andrew Newberg and Mark Robert Waldman, *Words Can Change
Your Brain: 12 Conversation Strategies to Build Trust, Resolve Conflict,
and Increase Intimacy* (New York: Penguin Press, 2012), 25.

19. Lizzie Velasquez, "To the Person Who Called Me 'the World's
Ugliest Woman' in a Viral Video," The Mighty, September 22,
2015, https://themighty.com/2015/09/lizzie-velasquez-response
-to-worlds-ugliest-woman-video/.

20. Lindsey Bever, "She Was Mocked for 'Looking Different.' Now
She Fights Bullying in SXSW Documentary," *Washington Post*,
March 16, 2015, https://www.washingtonpost.com/news/morning
-Mix/wp/2015/03/16/mocked-cruelly-by-millions-for-looking
-different-texas-woman-fights-bullying-in-sxsw-documentary/.

21. Anne Frank, *The Diary of a Young Girl* (City: Publisher, Year),
entry from March 7, 1944. Variant translation listed at https://
en.wikiquote.org/wiki/Anne_Frank.

Conclusion

1. Source for rat race quotation. Attributed to William Coffin.

2. Shannon L. Adler, "Quotable Quotes," accessed May 5, 2017,
http://www.goodreads.com/quotes/541070-you-are-not-what
-others-think-you-are-you-are.

3. Nobility quote citation here.

4. E. E. Cummings, *E. E. Cummings: A Miscellany,* ed. George James
Firmage (New York: Argophile Press, 1958), 13.

5. John Paul II, "Apostolic Visit to Toronto: Mass for the Seventeenth
World Youth Day" (homily, Downsview Park, Toronto, Canada,
July 28, 2002), https://w2.vatican.va/content/john-paul-ii/en/homilies
/2002/documents/hf_jp-ii_hom_20020728_xvii-wyd.html.

6. Albert Einstein, *The World as I See It* (1949; San Diego, CA:
The Book Tree, 2007), 2.

7. Attributed to Catherine of Siena.

8. Paul IV, "Address of Pope Paul IV to Women" (closing of the Second Vatican Ecumenical Council, December 8, 1965), https://w2.vatican.va/content/paul-vi/en/speeches/1965/documents/hf_p-vi_spe_19651208_epilogo-concilio-donne.html.